THE AMERICAS POETRY FESTIVAL OF NEW YORK 2015

MULTILINGUAL ANTHOLOGY

CARLOS AGUASACO & YRENE SANTOS (EDS)

artepoética
press

NUEVA YORK, 2015

Title: Multilingual Anthology: The Americas Poetry Festival of New York 2015

ISBN-10: 1940075378
ISBN-13: 978-1-940075-37-2

Design: © Ana Paola González
Cover & Image: © Jhon Aguasaco
Editor in chief: Carlos Aguasaco
E-mail: carlos@artepoetica.com
Mail: 38-38 215 Place, Bayside, NY 11361, USA.

© Multilingual Anthology: The Americas Poetry Festival of New York 2015, Carlos Aguasaco &
Yrene Santos (Eds)
© Multilingual Anthology: The Americas Poetry Festival of New York 2015, for this edition
Artepoética Press

MULTILINGUAL ANTHOLOGY

HONORS THE MEMORY OF POET
WILLIAM BELTRÁN
[AKA WILLIAM AKCOO 1973- 2011]

WWW.POETRYNY.COM

CONTENT

INTRODUCTION

For a second consecutive year, we celebrate The Americas Poetry Festival of New York. As a multilingual literary event, TAPFNY aims to celebrate all the cultures represented in New York and the Americas in general. Our city is simply the most diverse place in the world and therefore, our festival is bound to include an ever-increasing sample of the most diverse and admirable poetry on the planet. In 2014, we began with sixty poets representing fifteen countries and reading works in five languages. Now, in 2015, we have again invited sixty poets who represent a total of twenty one countries and are reading works in eight languages. Although we are proud of this increasing diversity, we have to recognize that the festival has a long way to go on its quest to fairly represent New York City's diverse population and cultural richness. On April 29, 2010, the New York Times reported that "while there is no precise count, some experts believe New York is home to as many as 800 languages"[1] and that students in the city's public school system speak 176 of them. We may never reach our goal, but we will certainly strive to accomplish it.

The festival is possible thanks to the generous support of The Division of Interdisciplinary Studies of The City College of New York (Center for Worker Education), the Walt Whitman Birthplace State Historic Site and Interpretive Center, the Americas Society / Council of the Americas AS/COA, The Consulate General and Promotion Center of the Argentine Republic in New York, and the newly formed Long Island Latino Arts Council. Artepoetica Press, Escribana Books and Terraza 7 have also joined this effort supporting the publication of this anthology.

Under the leadership of Dean Juan Carlos Mercado, The Division of Interdisciplinary Studies of The City College of New York has developed several forms of engaged scholarship aimed to better serve our students and the community. Besides this poetry festival, the Division of Interdisciplinary Studies celebrates the Americas Film Festival of New York (www.taffny.com) and has created the Master of Arts in the Study of the Americas (www.citycollegeamericasma.org).

The festival activities include multilingual poetry readings, round tables and academic conferences on contemporary poetry. This year we have programed two conferences by Professor Abeer Abdel Hafez, Chair of the Spanish Department at Cairo University, who will talk about Contemporary Egyptian

[1]   http://www.nytimes.com/2010/04/29/nyregion/29lost.html?_r=0

and Latin-American female poets, and Mexican editor and critic Margarita Monroy who will discuss the tunAstral movement. Our round table will center on the relationship between poetry and technology. Detailed information on these activities can be found in our website poetryny.com.

TAPFNY 2015 honors the memory of poet William Beltrán (a.k.a. William Akcoo, 1973-2011). William is one of the most independent and unique poetic voices of our times. He studied Art at the National University of Colombia and later moved to Spain where he attended the doctoral program in aesthetics at the Universidad Complutense de Madrid. A specialist in the philosophy of Nietzsche, William investigated deeply the relationship between art, volition and truth. He spoke Spanish, German and English and occasionally worked as an interpreter and as an art model while conducting his academic research in Germany. His written poetry (as he would have called it) is cryptic and to the point. It mainly delves into a critique of poetic prose and false modesty, but it also reveals the inner works of the artistic mind and its struggle to remain loyal to art as the ideal and probably the only pure form of existence. William rejected the concept of the modern subject, or the subject of modernity, and saw himself as a true "individual" immersed in a dialogue with poets such as Rimbaud, Baudelaire, and León de Greiff, among others. His early departure in 2011 kept him from finishing his novel *El abrazo de la perra muerta* (The Dead Bitch Embrace); also, most of his work remains unpublished. Those of us who had the honor of his friendship will always remember his authenticity and sincere love for poetry.

The present anthology only pretends to present a taste of the universe of the poets invited to TAPFNY 2015. The reader, hopefully, will find it as appealing as the festival itself and take it as an entrée to ignite further interest in the work of the featured poets.

Sincerely,

Carlos Aguasaco, Ph.D.
Assistant Professor, Latin American Cultural Studies & Spanish
Department of Interdisciplinary Arts & Sciences
City College of the City University of New York

ETNAIRIS RIBERA
[PUERTO RICO]

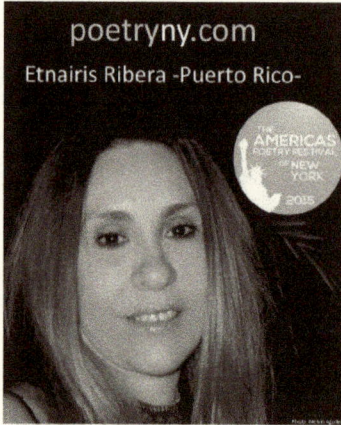

Etnairis Ribera, Puerto Rico, received the Great Literature Award 2008 for Lifetime Creative Excellence, PEN International-PR. Her work has been translated into English, Italian, French, Portuguese, Catalonian, Swedish, Arabic. She participates in international literature events and publishes in the Americas, Europe and Asia. Among her books: *A(MAR)ES, Ariadne of the Water, The birds of the goddess, Memoirs of a Poem and its Apple, Intervened, The voyage of the Kisses*. Ph. D. and Full Professor of Hispanic Literature, University of Puerto Rico. Thesis: *Mystical Poetics of Francisco Matos Paoli*, author who wrote the introduction to her youth book *Pachamamapa Taki (Song of Mother Earth)*, written in the Andes. She conducted the Puerto Rican Institute of Culture Poetry Workshop (2001-2002). Cultural activist, she leads the event *Caribbean Poetry* and is a founding member of the International Poetry Festival of Puerto Rico. Editor of *Dawning, Anthology in Homage of Julia de Burgos Centennial*.

EL HILO

Aquel laberinto lame sus adoquines.
Descubre el himen
y el espejo de unos lazos.

En la vieja ciudad, Ariadna
pasa entre sus muslos el hilo
antes de entregarlo como un mapa

y brinda por un nómada corazón,
por la esmeralda,
por las huellas encendidas del tigre.

El carnaval cuelga de los balcones,
mitad incógnita,
mitad de un viaje en el asombro.

THE THREAD

That labyrinth licks its cobblestones.
It discovers the hymen
and the mirrors of some laces.

In the old city, Ariadne
passes the thread between her thighs
before rendering it like a map
and toasts to a nomad heart, to the emerald,
to the tiger's shining footprints.

The carnival hangs from the balconies,
half unknown, half of an amazing voyage.

JANA PUTRLE SRDIĆ
[SLOVENIA]

poetryny.com
Jana Putrle Srdić —Slovenia—

Jana Putrle Srdić (Ljubljana, b. 1975) is a poet and intermedia art producer, occasional writer of film reviews and translator of poetry. She cooperated in different art projects, combining poetry with new media and published 3 poetry books: *Kutine* (Quinces, 2003); *Lahko se zgodi karkoli* (*Anything could happen*, 2007) and *To noč bodo hrošči prilezli iz zemlje* (*This night the beetles will come out of the ground*, 2014). The translated poetry books are entitled: *Puede pasar cualquier cosa* (Buenos Aires, 2011), *La noche en que los escarabajos surgieron de la tierra* (Madrid, 2015), and *Anything could happen* (New York, 2014). In numerous countries around the world (Europe, Russia, South America) she appeared on poetry festivals. She has translated poetry from English, Russian, Croatian and Serbian (Robert Hass, Sapphire, Ana Ristović, Contemporary Russian Poetry).

FISH

No matter how carefully you cut into the belly
of this wonderful silver fish and clean
the entrails, wipe the dust from the shelves,
and place fragile objects somewhere high,
safety will not save you from fear.
Misery doesn't ensure a good
poem. The closeness of death only makes you
more alone. Filled with joy, like an aquarium
with spawning fish,
we watch the ducks
follow one another with their shovel-like feet,
one two one two
in a line.
There is an order in everything,
some feathery lightness.

Translated by Barbara Jurša

RIBA

Če še tako previdno prerežeš trebuh
te čudovite srebrne ribe izvlečeš
drobovje obrišeš prah s poličk
in postaviš ostre predmete najviše
te varnost ne bo rešila strahov.
Beda ne zagotavlja dobre
pesmi. Bližina smrti te zgolj naredi bolj
samega. Napolnjeni z veseljem kot akvarij
z drstečimi ribami
gledamo race
ki si sledijo z zamahi lopatastih nog

en dva en dva
v vrsti.
Neki red je v vsem skupaj.
Neka peresna lahkost.

UN PEZ

Aun cuando le cortes con mucho cuidado la tripa
a este maravilloso pez plateado sacas
las entrañas quitas el polvo de las repisas
y pones los objetos frágiles más alto,
la seguridad no te salvará de los miedos.
La miseria no garantiza que un poema
sea bueno. La cercanía de la muerte sólo te hace más
solitario. Llenos de alegría, como un acuario
con peces que frezan,
miramos los patos
que se siguen uno al otro con brazadas de pies palmeados,
uno dos uno dos
en fila.
Hay un orden en todo esto.
Una ligereza de pluma.

Traducción de Barbara Pregelj

PAULO FERRAZ
[BRAZIL]

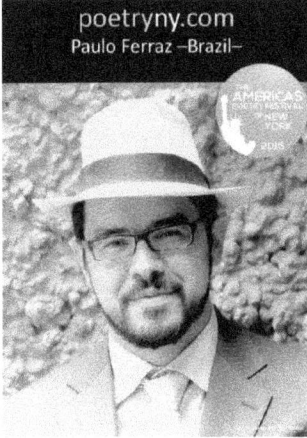

Paulo Ferraz (Rondonópolis, Brazil, 1974) is a poet, publisher and translator. He graduated from University of São Paulo (USP) with a bachelor's degree in Law and History. He continued his education, studying literary theory and getting a master's degree in Brazilian literature from the same university.

His first book, *Constatação do óbvio* (Selo Sebastião Grifo), was published in 1999. Eight years later, Ferraz put out a second and a third book, *Evidências pedestres* and *De novo nada* (Selo Sebastião Grifo). *De novo nada* was adapted to theatre in 2009 and translated into Spanish in 2011 with editions in Mexico and Ecuador.

He published a poetry magazine called *Sebastião* (2001 and 2002), and organized the anthology *Roteiro da poesia brasileira: anos 90* (2011). Ferraz has translated several poets from Spanish, Catalan and Russian to Portuguese and has been invited to participate in poetry readings in Monterrey, Oaxaca and Guadalajara (Mexico), Havana (Cuba), Barcelona (Spain), Guayaquil (Ecuador) and Lviv (Ukraine).

STILL LIFE

An oblique beam
a spotlight that
when turned onstage
hinder the eyes'

freedom, sliding

fluidly along
the canvas'
sterile surface
in small waves

that slowly wade
consuming the darkness
that surrounds them,
giving the impression

that inside a wicker
basket, on the veer
of the colors, apples
subject themselves to

time and rippen
to the dispair of a
mouth, ignorant of
the allure of linear
perspective (how can
the mind still fall for
the same everyday lie
that it eternally invents?)

Translatted by Matias Mariani

NATURALEZA MORTA

Uma luz oblíqua,
qual um holofote
que aceso no palco
tolhe a liberdade

dos olhos, desliza
líqüida por sobre a
superfície estéril
da tela em pequenas

vagas que vão lentas
erodindo o negro
que as envolve, dando a
nítida impressão que

dentro de uma cesta
de vime, na curva
das cores, maçãs se
sujeitam às leis do

tempo e amadurecem
para o desespero
da boca que ignora as
malícias do ponto

de fuga (como ainda a
mente cai na mesma
mentira de sempre
que ela pra si inventa?).

GUSTAVO TISOCCO
[ARGENTINA]

poetryny.com
Gustavo Tisocco –Argentina–

Gustavo Tisocco was born in Argentina, in the town of Mocoretá, province of Corrientes. He has published the following books of poetry: "Sutil" (*Subtle*), "Entre soles y sombras" (*Among Suns and Shadows*), "Paisaje de adentro" (*Interior Landscape*), "Pintapoemas" (*Paintpoems*); "Cicatriz" (*Scar*), "Rostro ajeno" (*Foreign Countenance*); "Desde todos los costados" (*From All Sides*), and "Terrestre" (*Earthly*), as well as the following CDs: "Huellas" (*Footprints*), "Intersecciones" (*Intersections*),"Corazón de níspero" (*Loquat Heart*), and "Terrestre" (*Earthly*). He has participated in various anthologies, both in Argentina and in other parts of the world. He has been invited to National and International Festivals. As Creator and Director of the MISPOETASCONTEMPORANEOS website, where he publishes the work of other poets for the past 9 years, he was honored with the Silver Puma Award granted by the Fundación Argentina para la Poesía (Argentine Poetry Foundation), among other awards. Some of his poems have been translated into Italian, Portuguese, Catalan, English, and French.

To write a ten acre poem
I will have to summon all the fish,
the magician who wanders through the nights,
the smell of freshly baked bread
the foam in the sea.

I will have to revive those who have left me,
bring back ships stranded in the breeze,
sapphires and emeralds,
the child that dreamed of being a scarecrow,
the old bell tower, the train platform in that village.

I will write my mother's name,
my people's ghosts,
a drop from the river, the caress from the willow.
From the tiniest herb its fragrance,
from the jigsaw puzzle its enigmas
and from the eyes of the departed his prayers.

A ten acre poem means feeling cold,
letting yourself go like a weathervane,
awakening in the tango that strips us bare,
being a kite, a mailbox, an archer.
Being dazzled by the stories of salt,
the flight of the humming bird,
and the statues in its cage.

That our country is wounded I must not forget,
that there are grandmothers still waiting and
an island full of gravestones and voices in the mist.
That the Crucified is still being crucified,
that so many wings are broken every day,
that we who spend our nights in the south are laughed at in the
north,

And when I fail to find words for those ten acres
I will turn to your name, your elfin feet,
your kiss, your sex erect,
your green gaze, your doubts and certainties,

your enchanted valley,
your insomnia, your alcohol.

Only there will the poem be born,
extended cry
true immortality.

Translation by Irene Marks

Para escribir un poema de diez hectáreas
tendré que convocar a todos los peces,
al mago que deambula en las noches,
al aroma de pan horneado,
a la espuma del mar.

Deberé resucitar a los que me dejaron,
retornar barcos encallados en la brisa,
zafiros y esmeraldas,
al niño que soñaba con ser espantapájaros,
al viejo campanario, al andén del pueblo aquel.

Pondré el nombre de mi madre,
los fantasmas de mi gente,
una gota de río, la caricia del sauce.
De la más ínfima hierba la fragancia,
del rompecabezas los enigmas
y de los ojos del ausente las plegarias.

Un poema de diez hectáreas insume tener frío,
dejarse llevar como una veleta,
despertar en el tango que nos desnuda,
ser cometa, buzón, arquero.
Que nos deslumbren los cuentos de sal,
el vuelo del colibrí,
y las estatuas en su jaula.

Que tenemos un país herido no debo olvidar,
que hay abuelas que esperan y
una isla llena de lápidas y voces en la bruma.
Que el Crucificado sigue siendo crucificado,
que se mutilan a diario tantas alas,
que se ríen en el norte de los que pernoctamos aquí en
el sur.

Y cuando me falten palabras para las diez hectáreas
acudiré a tu nombre, tus pies de duende,
a tu beso, tu sexo enhiesto,
tu mirada verde, a tus dudas y certezas,
a tu valle encantado,
a tu insomnio, a tu alcohol.

Sólo ahí nacerá el poema,
grito extendido
inmortalidad cierta.

AHMAD AL-SHAHAWY
[EGYPT]

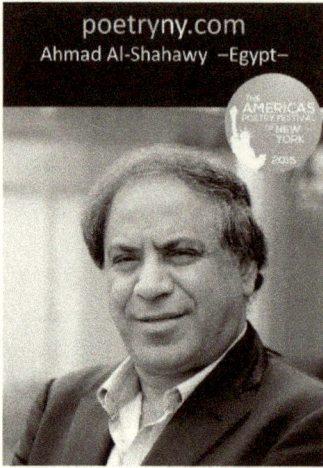

Born in Damietta, Egypt, 1960, Shahawy graduated from the Journalism Department, Sohag University, where he contributed to establishing a local newspaper. In 1985, he started working at the News Department of *Al Ahram* newspaper. He has been Managing Editor of *NISF ELDUNIA* – a weekly magazine published by Al-Ahram – since 1990. In 1991 he attended the International Writing Program in the United States. He was the recipient of UNESCO Literature Prize in 1995, and Cavafy Poetry Prize in 1998. The Rotterdam International Poetry Festival published two collections of the poet in English and Dutch in 2004. His poems have been translated into many languages including Turkish. Since 1987 he participated in many poetry festivals organized in many countries of the world. His published works: *Two Prayers for Love* (1998), *Conversations I-II* (1991, 1994), *States of the Lover* (1996), *Book of Death* (1997), Say That it is Her (2000), Water in the Fingers (2002), *The Commandments on the Love of Women* I-II (2003, 2006), *Tongue of the Fire* (2005), *One Gateway but So Many Abodes* (2009), *I Drive Clouds* (2010), *A Heaven in my Name* (2013). The translation of his last book into Turkish was published by Kırmızı Yayınları in 2014.

Ahmad is NOT His Name

A nouveau riche I am, I know;
I struck it rich and came upon me
a wealth so late,
but it did, at last
and hereby I make it
known to all:

in silence, I trade
and in tears as well:
I sell darkness
and make no profit at all;
I sell sleep for them
whose heads shine
with lanterns
that never go out.

I shroud defeats, however,
and corpses of memories
I burn, too,
for a very modest fee,
in order that lovers
may be oblivious,
and steal their souls
if they like it so.

I lend a triumph
to those who find hope
in the wildlife;
I barter certainty
for seclusions,
to those who've lost their teeth
in earthly ruptures,
not knowing yet
where Noah used to dwell.

I shall not lend at interest,
nor shall bargain,
or overprice,
even though we trade in
blame as pure as rain
and make an offer for
owners of the Elephant
so that they may not destroy
the Cube of love, again.

I trade in dust of graves
so that the dead
may remember less.
There is no room for mortgage
in my shops,
nor shelves for love,
since the one who sells
love in the marketplace
His name is not Ahmad.

Translated from Arabic by Bahaa-eddin M. Mazid

Translator's notes:

1. "blame as pure as rain " – Lit. "water of blame", citing a line of poetry by Abu
    Tammam.
2. "for Owners of the Elephant, so that they won't destroy the Cube of Love again" –
    an allusion to the Story of Elephant in the Quran. "Cube of Love" is a rendering of
    the Ka'aba of love, alluding to the Muslims' Holy Ka'aba in Mecca

María Negroni
[Argentina]

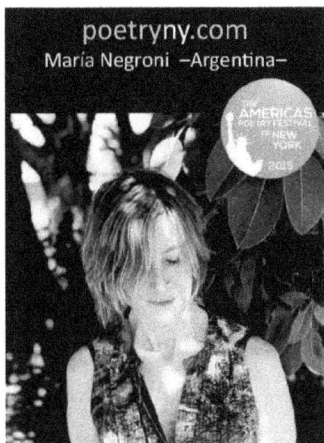

María Negroni (Rosario, Argentina) earned a PhD in literature from Columbia University. She has published numerous poetry collections including: *Islandia* (Monte Avila, 1994); *El viaje de la noche* (Lumen, 1994); *Arte y Fuga* (Pre-Textos, 2004), *Andanza* (Pre-Textos, 2009), *La Boca del Infierno* (Mantis, 2010), *Cantar la nada* (Bajo la Luna, 2011) and *Elegía Joseph Cornell* (Caja Negra, 2013). She has also published essays: *Ciudad Gótica* (Bajo la luna, 1994 y 2007), *Museo Negro* (Grupo Editorial Norma, 1999), *El testigo lúcido* (Beatriz Viterbo, 2003), *Galería Fantástica* (Premio Internacional de Ensayo, Siglo XXI, México) and *Pequeño Mundo Ilustrado* (Caja Negra, 2012); two novels: *El sueño de Ursula* (Seix-Barral, 1998) and *La Anunciación* (Seix-Barral, 2007). She has also published a book-object in collaboration with artist Jorge Macchi, Buenos Aires Tour (Ediciones Turner, Madrid 2004). Her latest book, *Cartas extraordinarias*, has just been released by Alfaguara, Buenos Aires 2013. Negroni is a worldwide renowned translator and has received the Guggenheim and Rockefeller fellowships among others. Her work has been translated to English, French, Italian and Swedish. Currently, she directs the Master in Creative Writing program at Universidad Nacional de Tres de Febrero in Buenos Aires.

ART AND FUGUE

IV
(canon inversus)

> *the rose is without a why*
> Angelus Silesius

a woman waits
on the riverbank
to say   what she doesn't know

and the river sees her and doesn't
and she
at a loss
about to find what she's looking for
a *that*
        she might possibly name
but doesn't dare
want

she sings

sings like falling asleep
in the lap of the water
that writes her

like calling
for her river body
choked with desire
in the hesitant night
        that arouses

and so
within limits
she awaits
    what she would hope
    to prefer

a liquid tremor
an unwarranted pain
expressible in the silence
        of that hovering music

she invents
to find out what she's saying
when she says
      I don't know

autumn onshore
openly night

there is no
other story

a woman invading
the unquiet page of desire
like a death attentive
      to the living
inside it

that impatience
to be what she would be
if the heart spoke out
orphaned and acceptant

the river sees her
      and then doesn't

and she
who doesn't know what the illusory
      house of things knew
without a why

she sings
now she's singing
      like taking flight
toward herself

and the river departs
written pain departs
      bearing with it her image
to the lands of the sea
where she hasn't
been born yet
      and is already a variant

Translated by Anne Twitty

IV
(canon inversus)

a rosa es sin por qué
Angelus Silesius

una mujer espera
a la orilla del río
para decir   lo que no sabe

y el río la ve y no la ve
y ella
en su desnuda inexperiencia
a punto de llegar a lo que busca
eso
    que tal vez podría decir
pero no sabe
querer

canta

canta como dormirse
en el regazo del agua
      que la escribe

como llamando
al río de su cuerpo
que calla de deseo
en la indecisa noche
      que lo inspira

y así
en la medida de las cosas
espera
      lo que ansiaría
      preferir

un líquido temblor
una música incumplida
      para saber qué dice
cuando dice
no saber

otoño en la ribera
abiertamente noche

no hay
más historia que ésta

una mujer que invade
la página nerviosa del deseo
como una muerte atenta
      a lo que vive
dentro de ella

esa impaciencia
por ser lo que sería
si el corazón hablara
tranquilo en su orfandad
y el río la ve
      y después no la ve

y ella
que ignora lo que supo
sin por qué
la inverosímil casa
de las cosas

canta
está cantando ahora
      como emprender un vuelo
hacia sí misma

y el río se va
se va la pena escrita
      llevándose su imagen
a las tierras del mar
donde ella todavía
no nació
      y es ya una desinencia

MICHAEL BRODER
[USA]

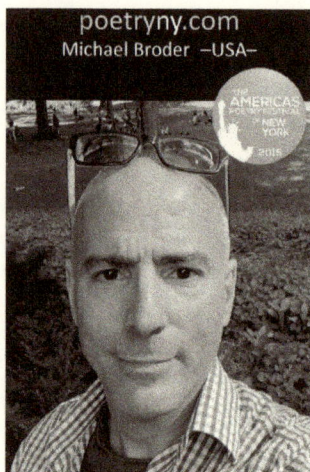

Michael Broder is the author of *This Life Now* (A Midsummer Night's Press, 2014), a finalist for the 2015 Lambda Literary Award for Gay Poetry. His poems have appeared in *American Poetry Review, Assaracus, BLOOM, Columbia Poetry Review, Court Green, Painted Bride Quarterly*, and other journals, as well as in the anthologies *This New Breed: Gents, Bad Boys* and *Barbarians 2* (Windstorm Creative, 2004), edited by Rudy Kikel; *My Diva: 65 Gay Men on the Women Who Inspire Them* (Terrace Books, 2009), edited by Michael Montlack; *Spaces Between Us: Poetry, Prose and Art on HIV/AIDS* (Third World Press, 2010), edited by Kelly Norman Ellis and ML Hunter; and *Divining Divas: 50 Gay Men on Their Muses* (Lethe Press, 2012), edited by Michael Montlack.

FROM THE HOTEL CUMDUMP NOTEBOOKS

* * *

This guy hits me up on Scruff.
Alex. Not his real name.
I know his real name now.
But I'll continue calling him Alex.
He didn't want to have sex with me.
He was about 90 miles away,
somewhere in New Jersey or Pennsylvania.
He just wanted to chat.
About being a cumslut.
Alex had been a more or less normal
gay man with a boyfriend.
More of a bottom,
but that's no special distinction.
Then he started to crave cum.
More than that, he started to crave HIV.
He wanted to get infected.
Some people call it "getting pozzed."
Alex says he started "chasing,"
short for "bug chasing,"
phrase from the 1990s
when some guys started
romanticizing HIV infection,
seeking HIV-positive partners
to bottom for raw,
hoping to get infected.
These bareback bottoms
were called bug chasers
The men who cooperated,
exposed them to HIV,
were called gift givers.
Sounds almost innocuous,
like straight, no chaser, or like
carelessly drinking from the same glass
as somebody with a bad cold.
There's so much more to it than that.

It is so deep and dark and damaged,
yet at the same time so completely
comprehensible, normal even.
Or so I say.
I know the idea that I find this
anything less than completely revolting
will itself seem completely revolting
to many people.
Are any of these people reading this poem?
I suppose some of them are.

Siomara España
[Ecuador]

poetryny.com
Siomara España —Ecuador—

Siomara España was born in 1976 in Manabí, Ecuador. España is a Poet and teacher of literature, aesthetics, and literary criticism at the University of Guayaquil. She is the Cultural editor of the newspapers *El Emigrante* and department director of the Casa de la Cultura Guayaquil. She has received several literary awards in Ecuador and Argentina. Published books: *Concupiscencia*; *Alivio demente*; *De cara al fuego Contraluz*; *El regreso de lolita*; *Jardines en el aire*; and *Construcción de los sombreros encarnados, música para una muerte inversa.* Her work has been translated and included in anthologies around the world.

WEDNESDAYS WOMAN

How often does the Wednesday woman
unfold her face
wash her feet
and walk again upon her words.
how often does she follow the same old path,
wander down the same old streets,
see the same traffic lights,
consider the same beggars, climb the same clouds,
seek out the same bed.
How often does the Wednesday woman
look for the mouth of her lover,
tremble in this arms,
and desperate cry out her love
and sob her words in silence.
How often does the Wednesday woman
want to flee her passion
forget her dreams
and simply stay tied down
how often does she laugh and sing
how many tears of love.
How often does the Wednesday woman
have to tie tight her soul
live her delirium and madness,
and walk again on what's been said,
walk again upon her words.

GABRIEL CHÁVEZ CASAZOLA
[BOLIVIA]

poetryny.com
Gabriel Chávez Casazola –Bolivia–

Gabriel Chávez Casazola (Bolivia, 1972) is a poet and journalist considered "an essential voice of the modern Bolivian and Latin American poetry." He published several books of poetry including *Lugar Común / Common Place* (1999), *Escalera de Mano / Stepladder* (2003), *El agua iluminada / Illuminated Water* (2010), and *La mañana se llenará de jardineros / The Morning will Bring out the Gardeners* (2013 in Ecuador; Second Edition in Bolivia, 2014). His work has been anthologized in different countries: *Camara de Niebla / Cloud Chamber* (El Suri Porfiado, Argentina, 2014), *El pie de Eurídice / the Foot of Eurydice* (Gamar, Colombia, 2014) and *La canción de la sopa / The Soup Song* (El Ángel, Ecuador, 2014).

Koyu Abe plants a sunflower seed in the gardens of the Temple of Genji

Koyu Abe, in a harsh black tunic,
head high and shaved
brow furrowed
plants a sunflower seed in the gardens of the Temple of Genji.

Unhurried, he buries the small shell full
of hidden light
of unfolding wonder
in a bowl dug from the Earth.

He covers it with a small shovel
waters it with orange sprinkles.

A breeze runs through the gardens of the Temple of Genji
Koyu Abe feels it on his hands sprayed with water.

In a bag made of fabric and hanging from his lap:
tens, hundreds of seeds.

It is still morning and his task is to plant each of these seeds
and to cover them
and to water them with orange sprinkles.

One million sunflowers should soon carpet the gardens of Genji and the
surrounding patches.

Monks, farmers,
all must have hands dampened by the water that irrigates the growing
yellow wonders of children:
these pious lights for exhausted eyes.

Koyu Abe does not know Van Gogh, but he paints sunflowers with his
shovel.
Koyu Abe, whose gaze descries, in the distance, the grayish profiles of
nuclear silos

On the edge of Fukushima rise the gardens of the Temple of Genji
and it is necessary to purify the heavens, purify the water, purify the soil,
purify the suns,
by the planting of sunflowers.

It is not about aesthetic effect—Koyu Abe speaks in the silence of the
image:
the roots absorb the heavy metals
and from the poison a flower is born.

But it is also true that beauty cleanses
itself,

says the Dutch, out of the silence of the fabric,
and Koyu Abe hands me a bag of seeds
shells filled with tiny light.

The vibrant orange shower
brings me closer to Van Gogh.

Translated from Spanish by M.J. Fievre

Koyu Abe siembra una semilla de girasol en los jardines del templo de Genji

Koyu Abe, con rigurosa túnica negra,
alta y rapada la cabeza
llano el ceño
siembra una semilla de girasol en los jardines del templo de Genji.

Con parsimonia deposita la pequeña cáscara repleta
de luz en potencia
de futuros asombros
en un cuenco cavado entre la tierra.

La cubre con una pequeña pala
la riega con una regadera anaranjada.

Pasa la brisa sobre los jardines del templo de Genji
la siente Koyu Abe en sus manos salpicadas por el agua.

En una bolsa de tela colgada en el regazo lleva
unas decenas o cientos de semillas.

Es aún muy de mañana y sembrar cada una es su tarea
y cubrirla
y regarla con su regadera anaranjada.

Un millón de girasoles habrán de alfombrar pronto los jardines de Genji
y los huertos aledaños.

Monjes, campesinas,
todos habrán de tener manos humedecidas por el agua que riega los
futuros
asombros amarillos de los niños,
las que serán luces piadosas para ojos extenuados.

Koyu Abe no conoce a Van Gogh, mas pinta girasoles con su pala.
Koyu Abe, cuya mirada divisa, en lontananza, los perfiles grisáceos de los
silos nucleares.

A la vera de Fukushima se levantan los jardines del templo de Genji
y es preciso purificar el cielo, purificar las aguas, purificar el suelo,
purificar los soles sembrando girasoles.

No es un efecto estético, me dice Koyu Abe, en el silencio de la imagen:
las raíces absorben los metales pesados
y del veneno nace, como si tal, la flor.

Mas es verdad que también la belleza purifica
por sí misma,

acota el holandés, saliendo del silencio de la tela,
y Koyu Abe me extiende una bolsa de semillas
de cáscaras repletas de diminuta luz.

La enorme regadera anaranjada
me la alcanza Van Gogh.

JAIME MANRIQUE
[COLOMBIA/USA]

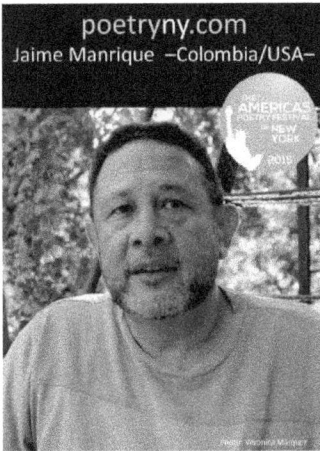

Jaime Manrique is a Colombian-born novelist, poet, essayist, and translator who has written both in English and Spanish, and whose work has been translated into fifteen languages. Among his publications in English are the novels *Colombian Gold, Latin Moon in Manhattan, Twilight at the Equator, Our Lives Are the Rivers* and *Cervantes Street*; the volumes of poetry *My Night with Federico García Lorca*; *Tarzan, My Body, Christopher Columbus*; and the memoir *Eminent Maricones: Arenas, Lorca, Puig, and Me*. His honors include Colombia's National Poetry Award, 2007 International Latino Book Award (Best Novel, Historical Fiction), and a Guggenheim Fellowship. Manrique's *Selected Poems* in Spanish will appear in Colombia in 2016. He's a former Associate Professor in the MFA in writing at Columbia University and currently a Distinguished Lecturer in the Department of Modern Languages and Literature in the City College of New York. He has just completed *Two Men*, a new novel.

In memoriam, Josefina Folgoso

ANGRY

with death
that has taken
Josefina, I grab
a pair of scissors
at dusk
and attack
the perfumed stems
of white bells
of basil on my porch
that, in the pregnant days
of August, attract stingers
and legions of tiny
honey bees. In the engulfing
darkness, I cut
the stems and make
a bouquet for you,
dear friend,
who died much too soon when
so many other things
take too long to die.
Let the bees go
and feed elsewhere—
not on my porch, where I mourn
you with rage.
Who needs bees,
I fume as I cut
the sweet basil flowers
to adorn my grief.

A Josefina Folgoso, *in memoriam*

FURIOSO

con la muerte
que se llevó
a Josefina, agarro
las tijeras
al atardecer
y ataco
los racimos perfumados
de campanas blancas
de la albahaca en mi terraza
que en los días preñados
de agosto atraen avispas
y legiones de diminutas
abejas preparando la miel.
En la oscuridad que me abraza
corto los gajos y hago
un ramillete para ti,
amiga querida,
muerta con demasiada premura
cuando tantas otras cosas
se demoran una eternidad para irse.
¡Que se larguen las abejas
con su miel a otra parte!
Nos las quiero en mi terraza,
digo entre dientes.
¿Quién necesita abejas?
Me quejo con amargura mientras corto
las dulces flores de albahaca
para adornar mi pena.

TINA ESCAJA
[SPAIN]

poetryny.com
Tina Escaja —Spain—

Tina Escaja is a Spanish author, digital artist and scholar based in Burlington, Vermont. As a literary critic, she has published extensively on gender and contemporary Latin American and Spanish poetry and technology. Her creative work transcends the traditional book form, leaping into digital art, video and multimedia projects exhibited in museums and galleries in Spain, Mexico and the United States. In 2003 she was awarded the International Poetry Prize "Dulce María Loynaz" for her manuscript Caída Libre, published in 2004. Other poetry titles include 13 lunas 13 (2011), Código de barras (2007), and Respiración mecánica (2001/2014). Escaja's experimental and hypertextual works include the poetic artifacts Negro en Ovejas (2011), VeloCity (2000-2002), Código de barras (2006), and the interactive novel Pinzas de metal (2003). Her poetry has been translated into six languages and has appeared in literary collections around the world. A selection of Escaja's literary and digital projects can be experienced at www.tinaescaja.com

DEATH ARRIVES IN TWO, winter arrives
and the end of the days,
your arrival arrives.
The end comes suctioned by the eye of a fleshless god,
of a cruel and obsolete god that masturbates sea swells and smashes
the world of the enormous city in two.
Devouring it.

And you arrive as well, adventuress, with your pink belly and your
clitoris to be made,
with your tender marmalade of a body at conception.
Liberated from wise men, from messiahs, from revelations.

And the world succumbs its all to the declaration of god,
of that god with no memory, with no more direction than a phallus
sucked by masses that inherit him,
with less itinerary
than a crazy confused prophet perpetuated in dildos and charms.
You arrive on time love,

if by chance I survive the assault.

English translation by Mark Eisner

LLEGA LA MUERTE A DOS, llega el invierno
y el final de los días
y tu llegada llega.
Llega el fin succionado por el ojo de un dios sin carne,
de un dios obsoleto y cruel que masturba oleajes y rompe el mundo
en dos de la ciudad enorme.
La devora.

Y tú llegas también, aventurera, con tu vientre rosa y tu clítoris por
hacer,
con esa tierna mermelada tuya de cuerpo a concebir.
Liberada de sabios, de mesías, de revelaciones.

Y el mundo sucumbe todo al alegato de dios,
de ese dios sin memoria, sin más rumbo que un falo succionado por
masas que lo heredan,
sin más itinerario
que un profeta loco y confundido perpetuado en dildos y amuletos.

Llegas a tiempo amor,

si acaso sobrevivo la embestida.

Juan Armando Rojas Joo
[Mexico]

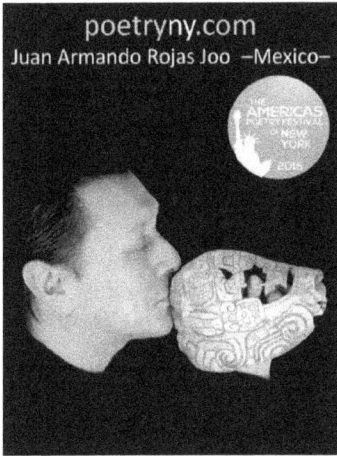

poetryny.com
Juan Armando Rojas Joo —Mexico—

Juan Armando Rojas Joo is a transborder poet, narrator and essayist. Rojas' books include: *Luz / Light* (2013), *Vertebral River / Río vertebral (2009, 2002)*, *Ceremonial of Wind / Ceremonial de viento (2006)*, *Santuarios desierto mar (2004)* and *Lluvia de lunas (1999)*. Rojas has co-edited the anthologies *Sangre mía / Blood of Mine: Poetry of Border Violence, Gender, and Identity in Ciudad Juárez* (2013), and *Canto a una ciudad en el desierto* (2004), poetic denouncements against feminicide. During the spring of 2011 Rojas was honored by the Universade de Coimbra, Portugal, as the resident poet. Rojas completed his Ph.D. at the University of Arizona in 2002 and was the Andrew W. Mellon Fellow at Amherst College, Massachusetts, and currently teaches at Ohio Wesleyan University where he chairs the Department of Modern Foreign Languages.

Spanish 1070

(16/IX/10)

> *"For everyone, everything, for us, nothing"*
> Subcomandante Marcos

I should say, that in this place, amongst other things I teach students grammar. When the course begins we review the present tense:

I open the door/ you are silent / he points his gun at me/ that we are what?/ and you all don't say anything/ when they are ready to shoot me.

Days later I teach my students the art of contrasting the preterit and the imperfect. They practiced the language that was taught here:

I opened the door/ you were silent/ he pointed his gun at me/ we…used to be/ we … were?/ you all did not say anything when they were ready to fire.

Time runs by –like it tends to do–and life gets so complicated that it reaches the point of the subjunctive. The students are graded according to their oral ability:

Open the door!/ You, I already told you, shut up!/ … because its possible that he will point his gun at my head/ given that perhaps we (the other) are thieves and you all are quiet (just in case)/ when they are ready to open fire on me/ with their five weapons pointing at my head.

I should say that I am a Spanish professor and that amongst other things, of course, I teach Spanish. When the course ends the students use the language/ –I write (on my knees and handcuffed) on the ground/ you, the police man tells me, shut up!/ perhaps I should open the door/ so that he can point his gun in my face/ don't shoot its my office!/ that I/you/he/she and we/ when you/not us if they/ the other history/the most official version/ so that (you all/ them) will not forget/ since the power that protects them forces us/ we, if an apology never comes… shut up or I'll arrest you!/ Or you shoot me?/ because this bitter shot/ you either drink it or you spill it/ (on my knees and you/he/we/you all/ them/ confused)/because when I see the barrel of the gun/ –so cold and cruel/ the law will take its silence to the grave.

Translated by Jennifer Rathbun

Español 1070

(16/IX/10)

> *"Para todos, todo, para nosotros, nada"*
> Subcomandante Marcos

Debo decir que, en este lugar, entre otras cosas enseño gramática a los estudiantes.Al iniciar el curso repasamos el tiempo presente:

Yo abro la puerta/ tú guardas silencio/ él me apunta con su revolver/ ¿que nosotros somos qué?/ y ustedes no dicen nada/ cuando ellos están a punto de dispararme.

Días después enseño a mis alumnos el arte de contrastar el pretérito y el imperfecto. Ellos practicaban el lenguaje que aquí se les enseñó:

Yo abrí la puerta/ tú guardabas silencio/ él me apuntó con su revólver/ nosotros... éramos/ ¿nosotros... fuimos?/ ustedes no dijeron nada cuando ellos estaban a punto del disparo.

El tiempo corre —como suele suceder— y las cosas en la vida se complican, hasta el subjuntivo. Los alumnos reciben notas de acuerdo a su destreza oral:

¡Abra la puerta!/ Tú, ya te lo dije, ¡que guardes silencio!/ … porque es probable que él apunte con su arma en mi cabeza/ ya que quizás crean que nos/otros somos ladrones y ustedes callen (por si acaso)/ cuando ellos estén a punto del disparo/ con sus cinco armas de fuego a mi cabeza.

Debo decir que profesor de lenguas soy y que entre otras cosas, claro está, enseño español. Al terminar el curso los alumnos usan el lenguaje/ –escribo yo (hincado y esposado) sobre el suelo/ tú, me dice el policía, ¡guarda silencio!/ quizás yo deba abrir la puerta/ para que él apunte su revólver en mi rostro/ ¡que no dispare es mi oficina!/ ya que yo/tú/ él/ella y nosotros/ cuando ustedes/ jamás nosotros si ellos/ la otra historia/ la versión más oficial/ para que (ustedes/ ellos) no la olviden/ ya que el poder que les protege nos obliga/ a nosotros, si el perdón, nunca vendrá... ¡guarda silencio o te arresto!/ ¿o me disparas?/ porque este amargo trago/ o te lo bebes o lo derramas/ (yo hincado y tú/ él/ nosotros/ ustedes/ ellos/ confundido/s)/ cuando del arma la mira miro/ –tan fría y cruel/ la ley defiende a muerte su silencio.

MERCEDES ROFFÉ
[ARGENTINA]

One of the most renowned contemporary Latin American poets, Mercedes Roffé was born in Buenos Aires, Argentina. She has lived in New York City since 1995. Widely published in Latin America and Spain, some of her books have been published in translation in Italy, Quebec, Romania, and England. Her poetry collection, *La ópera fantasma* (Madrid/México, Vaso Roto, 2012) was chosen one of the best books of 2012 by two major Mexican newspapers. Her book *Las linternas flotantes* (2009) translated as *Floating Lanterns* by Anna Deeny has been published by Shearsman Books (Bristol, UK, 2015). Her most recent poetry collection is entitled *Carcaj: Vislumbres* (Madrid/México, Vaso Roto, 2014).

She is the founding editor of Ediciones Pen Press (www.edicionespenpress.com), a New York-based independent press dedicated to the publication of contemporary poetry from around the world. Roffé holds a diploma in Modern Languages from the University of Buenos Aires, and a Ph.D. from New York University. She was awarded a John Simon Guggenheim Fellowship (2001) and a Civitella Ranieri Foundation Fellowship (2012).

BREAKING THE VICIOUS CYCLE

My fate

       to carry in my soul a white,

barren forest

in my eyes, nothingness

and in my hands, the loop that will choke me

a nest on my head commands me
to be born from myself

a crow, meanwhile
waits for dawn
for the spell brewed by his gaze and mine
to break

English translation by Judith Filc

ROMPIENDO EL CÍRCULO VICIOSO

Mi sino

       llevar en el alma un bosque

blanco, estéril

en los ojos, la nada

y en las manos, el aro que me ahorque

un nido en la cabeza me conmina
a nacer de mí

un cuervo, mientras tanto
espera que amanezca
que se rompa el hechizo que conjugan
su mirada y la mía

Mónica González Velázquez
[Mexico]

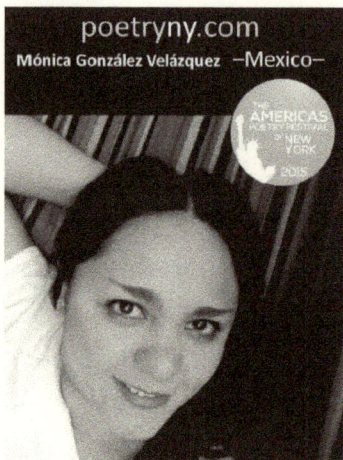

poetryny.com
Mónica González Velázquez —Mexico—

Mónica González Velázquez (Mexico City, 1973). She studied graphic design at the La Escuela Nacional de Artes Plásticas (UNAM) and has a diploma in Literry Creation from SOGEM. She has published nine books: *Tríptico de desamor, La luz y las sombras altas, Poesía Reunida, Las cosas últimas, Gran mal, Glory box* (republished in Ecuador); *Las eternas rutas, Le mystère de la vulgaire mondes* and *Breviario de la Renunciación.* Her visual poetry is included in the anthology *La palabra transfigurada. 100 años de poesía visual mexicana.* In 2010 she was awarded a grant from the Spanish Agency for International Development Cooperation. She is the publisher of miCielo ediciones.

Inventory and Farewell

I

I look at the horizon, I descend. A reddish sky blankets the city; so often hated-loved-hated, and fleeting yearning of one who has never walked it. On the periphery of these jaws that devour, chew and digest without distinction; at the height of horizontal life, my belonging dwell: a half-read book (between sleep, twilight and moments of waiting), a vast collection of intermittent syncopes (voices and metallic sounds that enliven the afternoon), a bed (where at certain hours, miracles are possible and pacts of peace have been signed, there is no hunger or sickness and children are not the target of extremist attacks, and whoever walks does so with the spirit), a pillow (where both the fury of so many days of aggressive activism and the echo of the libertarian shout from the jungle might rest), a table that seats four, a lily at its center and space to share food and heart; which is also included in the inventory alongside a pair of legs that transport it and hands that cool it, a pair of eyes that watch it beat despite the horror and the spilt blood (but that's what we're primarily made from: blood, bones, pain) beside the pain dwells hope, a pair of suitcases, traveling shoes for the journey and unimaginable landscapes in this place where the roads diverge.

II

Now that you're finally leaving, leave me on the side of the road facing forward. Leave me with the beastiary that dwells in my dreams and my men and my women and my machine of forgetting and my family history and my laces in my shoes and my errors and my few good decisions and my voice cutting the air, when nothing is enough now and only the Blues console me. Leave me with my posters: Goya, Tapies, Bacón, Modigliani. Leave me with Miller's vertigoes and a gravely ill Gil de Biedma resting on the nightstand. Leaveme with Luis Urbina: *Llora y llora, con su amor como un pájaro loco, dando tumbos en la noche estrellada.* Leave me with anxieties, the floor padded floor, lips and heart clenched; love bites in the mouth's cavity and nameless so-white lips.

But above all other things, leave me with my dose of reality and a glass of water in my hand.

Translated from Spanish by Lawrence Schimel

EL INVENTARIO Y LA DESPEDIDA

I

Miro el horizonte, desciendo. Un cielo rojizo tapiza la ciudad; tantas veces odiada–amada–odiada, y anhelo fugaz de quien jamás la haya caminado. En la periferia de esta fauce que engulle, mastica y digiere sin distinción; en lo más alto de la vida horizontal, habitan mis pertenencias: un libro a medio leer (entre el sueño, el ocaso y los turnos de espera), una vasta colección de síncopas intermitentes (voces y sonidos metálicos que dan vida al atardecer), una cama (donde a ciertas horas, los milagros son posibles y los pactos de paz han sido firmados, no hay hambre, enfermedad y los niños no son el blanco de ataques extremistas, y el que camina lo hace con el espíritu), una almohada (donde reposa la furia de tantos días de activismo combativo y el eco del grito libertario desde la selva), sábanas blancas (donde los ángeles copulan), una mesa con cuatro plazas, un lirio en su centro y espacio para compartir las viandas y el corazón; quien también consta en el inventario junto con un par de piernas que lo transportan y unas manos que lo entibian, un par de ojos que lo miran latir a pesar del horror y la sangre derramada –pero de eso estamos hechos principalmente: sangre, huesos, dolor– al lado del dolor habita la esperanza, un par de maletas, zapatos de viaje para la travesía y paisajes inimaginables en este sitio donde los caminos bifurcan.

II

Ahora que por fin te vas, déjame al lado de la carretera y con la boca por delante. Déjame con el bestiario que habita en mis sueños y mis hombres y mis mujeres y mi máquina de olvido y mi historia de familia y mis cuerdas en los zapatos y mis errores y mis pocos aciertos y mi voz cortando el aire, cuando ya nada es suficiente y sólo me consuela el Blues. Déjame con mis afiches: Goya, Tapies, Bacón, Modigliani. Déjame con los vértigos de Miller y Gil de Biedma severamente enfermo, reposando en la mesilla de noche. Déjame con Luis Urbina: *Llora y llora, con su amor como un pájaro loco, dando tumbos en la noche estrellada.* Déjame con ansias, el piso alfombrado, los labios, el corazón apretado; mordiscos en la cavidad de la boca y unos labios blanquísimos sin nombre.

Pero sobre todas las cosas, déjame con mi dosis de realidad y un vaso de agua en la mano.

ALEX LIMA
[ECUADOR]

Alex Lima is the author of two poetry collections, *Inverano* (2008) and *Bilocaciones* (2011). His poems have also appeared in literary magazines and anthologies home and abroad. He currently resides in Long Island where he works as Adjunct Instructor of Spanish at Suffolk County Community College (SUNY). Mr. Lima is an active member of the art collective We Are You Project International and co-founder of the Latino Arts Council of Long Island. He received his Ph.D. from the City University of New York (The Graduate Center) with a dissertation on the Jesuit poet Juan Bautista Aguirre (1725-1786). His new book, *Alba*, will be published by Artepoética Press, New York.

72 GENERATIONS

between you and I
hot climate, cold climate
good hair, bad hair
light skin, dark skin
protection from the cold
protection from the sun
spiky hair for sweat
running down my neck
straight hair for the winter cold
freezing down your ears and temples
dark eyes to filter luminosity
light eyes for longer winter nights
extra melanin but less Vitamin D
thick eyebrows to wipe off sweat in the fields
full lips to kiss goodbye all prejudice
why do you have to be what you eat
when you can be whatever you choose to be?
Despite our differences
most of us in this room are less that ten
generations apart
Reach out!
each generation gap
is only a handshake away.

Ana Luisa Martínez
[Dominican Republic-]

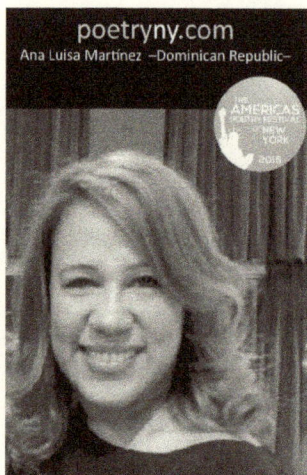

poetryny.com
Ana Luisa Martínez –Dominican Republic–

Ana Luisa Martínez (Santiago, Dominican Republic). A resident of New York since 1991, Ana Luisa is a graduate of John Jay College of Criminal Justice in New York City with a Bachelor's Degree in Criminal Justice. She is currently pursuing a Master's Degree in Advanced Spanish and Hispanic American Literature Studies at Universidad de Barcelona (with a projected graduation date of summer, 2016). She is the co-founder of Fundación Profesor Juan Bosch-USA. Her work appears in anthologies in the United States of America and El Salvador. She has participated in a number of literary events including the Dominican Book Fair in New York, the Women Writers Fair of the Dominican Women's Development Center, Lawrence International Book Fair (Massachusetts) and the International Congress of Writers and Literary Groups of Sosúa, Dominican Republic.

GARDEN OF THE LUMPEN GODS

1

Between the tongue and second heaven
vermin multiply
and the dew perverts as it falls.
Every race bows prostrate
before the same courtesan with the loose-fitting crown
under whose skirt lies concealed the rot
of a mediocre world.
The same woman rises arrogant
on the banks of the Seine,
Mrs. Starbucks' twin.
From Rome (the Great)
to the Restored One
the peacocks of phonetics
flock together and reply
with images that play out behind our backs.
Adulterous gods of noble stock with a shattering song
and living quarters of which GOD does not partake.

2

Angels
and demons,
fearing fate,
sketch other masks for themselves.
Mankind, meanwhile, saps the strength of silence
with the wan joy of its feeling understood
and flourishes to the ice bucket challenge
in the garden of these lumpen gods.
I wonder:
how many Decembers will we see naked
before stirring underbrush and digging up roots?

3

We are fugitive bodies
under the spell of these gods' absolution.
Let us cut the threads that pass through the eyes
of the beads on our necklaces made of metal, living quarters and titles
which, amid broken lives, keep us eagerly waiting!

Translated from Spanish by Walter Krochmal

JARDÍN DE LOS DIOSES VULGARES

1

Entre la lengua y el segundo cielo
se acrecientan alimañas
y pervierte el rocío al caer.
Cada raza se postra
ante la misma cortesana de corona suelta,
bajo cuya falda se esconde la fetidez
de un mundo mediocre.
La misma mujer que se levanta, arrogante,
a orilla del *Sena,*
gemela de la señora *Starbucks.*
Desde Roma (la grande)
hasta la Restaurada,
los pavorreales de la fonética
se auto-organizan y contestan
con imágenes que se despliegan a nuestras espaldas.
Dioses adúlteros de linaje, con canto que sacude
y morada donde DIOS no comulga.

2

Ángeles
y demonios
por temor al destino
se bosquejan otras máscaras.

Mientras, el hombre le quita fuerza al silencio
con su vago goce de creerse comprendido.
Y florece a cubo de agua fría
en el jardín de estos dioses vulgares.
Me pregunto,
¿cuántos diciembres veremos al desnudo
antes de revolver maleza y esculcar raíces?

3

Somos cuerpos fugados
bajo el hechizo de la absolución de estos dioses.
¡Quebremos los hilos que enhebran
las cuentas de nuestros collares de metales, moradas y títulos
que entre vidas rotas, nos mantienen en espera!

AUGUSTA EUNICE CASTILLO
[DOMINICAN REPUBLIC]

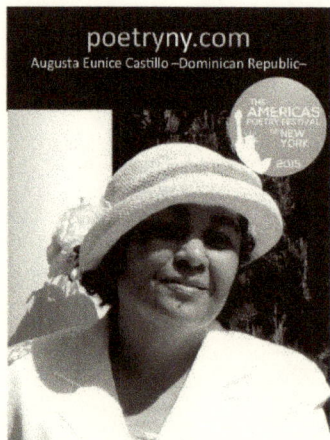

Augusta Eunice Castillo Ahmad is a Dominican – fine artist and a poet who lives in N.Y. City. She studied at Colegio Mary Lithgow & Jose Dubeau in Puerto Plata, her hometown. Eunice took several courses in fashion design at Pratt Institute N.Y. and holds a Masters degree in Fine Arts form CUNY where she worked as a monitor as well as a tutor for the SEEK Program. She was honored with the Charles Shaw & Bernard Horlick awards. Eunice holds a Masters Degree in Education from Long Island University, and teaches English as a Second Language. Secretos del faro is her first poetry book. La huella de Manuela obtained an honorary mention from Letras de Ultramar Contest, and it was published by Comisionado Dominicano de Cultura U. S. A. Her poems appear on Mujeres de Palabra Poetic Anthology. She is a member of Golden Key Honor Society and the literary workshop Camila Henríquez Ureña N.Y.

MACHO DE QUÉ

Cuándo se ahogará el furor
que esperma tu alevosía
encima de Ella

Qué colinas libaron tus entrañas
para amamantarte la vida,
Macho por quién
cómo asfixias el náhuatl
cuando tomas posesión de los pezones
que mueren a mordiscos,
hijo de cuándo
por dónde habrá abortado tu grito de luz
Perpleja ante tu perfidia
la tiara contempla
al tul que se ciega sobre unos ojos
maquillados con sangre
mientras seduces al gatillo
huyendo con el pensamiento entre las piernas,
Macho de nada;
te cuelga el alma
más abajo del raciocinio que te blasfema

Macho del Samalayuca
qué cactus de barril
reemplazará tu conciencia
cuando embriagas a la piel zagala
para clavarle tu botella
en su pudor;
Macho de qué
poblado del desierto

Macho de quién
cuántas lágrimas hembras
degüella tu hombría entre bigotes
Macho por dónde

Macho de entonces
qué memoria tendrá tu costilla
cuando despiertes.

CARLOS VELÁSQUEZ
[COLOMBIA]

Carlos Velásquez PhD. (Colombia, Bogotá, 1969). Poet, translator, musician and scholar. He attended Universidad Nacional de Colombia where he studied both music and literature. He latter received a Master degree in Latin American Literature from the University of Washington in Seattle. Carlos earned his PhD at the University of Arizona where he specialized in the study of film and literature. He taught at Bowling Green State University and is currently a visiting assistant professor at New Mexico Highlands University. He has published two poetry collections *Vesos del insilio* (1999) & *Es de tontos el regreso* (2004). This year Artepoerica Press will release his translation and edition of Seamus Scanlon's *As Close as You'll Ever Be.* His academic study *Pliegues cinematográficos. La función barroca en el cine hispanoamericano contemporáneo* will be published by Escribana Books in 2016.

YA MIS ARMAS HAN CAÍDO

Mi pecho sudoroso resopla
La angustia del pronto deceso
Has de aligerar tu carga
Pues no hay bastimento
Ni paciencia
Para soportar la rémora
De los vencidos

Empuña la lanza

Que tus acerados músculos
Rasguen el aire
Y el zumbido veloz
De la fraguada pica
Sea la fanfarria postrera
De mis carnes laceradas
Por el llamado de la muerte

No mires tras de mí
Bástete este ser que se ofrenda
Y no busques tras mi sombra
Pues tan sólo hallarás
A quienes me enviaron a tu encuentro
Y de mí retienen acaso
El fulgor de un recuerdo
Turbio en el destierro de su memoria
Aún más lejano que la esperanza perdida

Aquellas figuras
Que ves
Como lóbrega extensión
Tras de mi sombra
Me han lanzado a tu presencia
Sin más escudo que mis ojos
Y mi boca
Las armas más tenaces

Y también las más temerarias
Pero ni así la victoria
Vino a tropezar
Con mi trasegar perdido

Reúne entonces el vigor de tu cuerpo
Y arroja la pértiga
Como si desearas romper
De un solo tajo la densidad de la noche
Pues mi vida
Ahora no vale más
Que el susurro de mi último aliento
No te lo impida pudor alguno
Que ya no hay sustento esencial
Para mi canto

Si fui guerrero
Me he extraviado
Y aunque mis pasos
Buscaron muchas sendas
El destino de la derrota
Impávido me condujo a esta arena
Si mi nombre fue legión
Ahora no queda más que la soledad infinita
Al abrigo de mi agonía

No mires más
Tras de esta lúgubre sombra
Ya la noche me cobija
Y se hace tarde para tu regreso

Carolina Zamudio
[Argentina]

poetryny.com
Carolina Zamudio –Argentina–

Carolina Zamudio was born in Curuzú Cuatiá, Corrientes, Argentina, in 1973. She is a poet and journalist, and holds a Master's degree in Institutional Communications and Public Affairs. La Nación, a daily from Argentina, awarded her the 21st Century College Students Prize. She is the author of *Seguir al viento* [Following the Wind]. She has been included in several anthologies. Her work has been partially translated into several languages. Her latest book *La oscuridad de lo que brilla / The Darkness of What Shines* will be realased by Artepoetica Press in the fall 2015.

CERTAINTY

Death cannot be lamented through swirls of certainty.

It happens (almost always) in the midst of outbursts
From one joy to the next
It falls silent and breeds in the heart of fear.
Life is a crack of light
Flowing from the purest black
To endless darkness.
We live firing up rattles for ourselves
We don't cry because we're speechless
And (like music from empty boxes)
We'd like to shed our bodies looking for relief.
Death is out there mocking
Goading that thing we call absence
Ordering others to clothe the body.

We then fear not to be touched
Or hugged anymore by our children.
We guess, belatedly, other endings
Like owners of that life we shared
(Time and space).
We run away, we duck
Arrogantly, helplessly, we refuse to move
From our own lives.
If by any chance I could stifle that face
That doesn't cry or musters up arguments:
Before us, the others
And the only one with a certainty.

We think we live
A convulsion
A short circuit
A heart attack in a race interrupted by the dream
Like that one from which we awake
Wondering if it is true
If we're still alive

Or if perhaps we were us.
And we discover that death can be
That luminous moment
That happens after the black, long while
That someone named life.

Death lives and is the only certainty.

CERTEZA

La muerte no se llora en remolinos de certeza.

Sucede –casi siempre– en medio de arrebatos
de una alegría a otra
se calla y fecunda en el centro del miedo.
La vida es una grieta de luz
que transcurre entre el negro más puro
a la oscuridad infinita.
Vivimos encendiéndonos estertores
no lloramos porque estamos mudos
y –como música de cajas huecas–
queremos escapar del cuerpo buscando alivio.
La muerte anda por ahí burlona
aguijonea eso que nombramos ausencia
es quien manda a otros a que vistan el cuerpo.

Entonces tememos no ser rozados
abrazados ya por nuestros hijos.
Conjeturamos, tarde, otros finales
como dueños de esa vida que compartimos
–tiempo y espacio–.
Huimos, esquivamos
nos plantamos arrogantes desvalidos
ante nuestra propia vida.
Si acaso contuviera ese mohín

que no llora o se llena de argumentos:
ante nosotros, los otros
y el único con una certeza.

Creemos vivir
un espasmo
un cortocircuito
un infarto en la carrera entrecortada por el sueño
como ese del que despertamos
preguntándonos si es cierto
si seguimos vivos
o acaso fuimos nosotros.
Y descubrimos que la muerte puede ser
ese instante luminoso
que sucede tras el negro y largo rato
que alguien nombró vida.

La muerte vive y es la única certeza.

DANIEL SHAPIRO
[USA]

Daniel Shapiro is the author of the poetry collections *Child with a Swan's Wings* (2013), *The Red Handkerchief and Other Poems* (2014), and "Woman at the Cusp of Twilight" (forthcoming). His translation of Chilean poet Tomás Harris's *Cipango* (2010) received a starred review in *Library Journal*. His poetry, prose, and translations have been published widely in journals including *American Book Review*, *The American Poetry Review* (cover feature, Tomás Harris), *Black Warrior Review*, *BOMB*, and *The Brooklyn Rail*, and in the anthologies *Mexico: A Traveler's Literary Companion*, *Vapor Transatlántico/Tramp Steamer*, and *The Oxford Book of Latin American Poetry*. He has received fellowships from the National Endowment for the Arts and PEN to translate Roberto Ransom's *Desaparecidos, animales y artistas* (Missing Persons, Animals and Artists). Shapiro serves as Director of Literature and Editor of *Review: Literature and Arts of the Americas* at the Americas Society in New York.

SUMMER, GUADALAJARA

Güero danced a drunk bolero on the roof.
He gave me a peso crushed smooth
by a train, a green clay figurine.

We swam in the fountain, circled by cars;
drivers stopped to whistle:
gringo. Güero shouted back, *no, francés*,
water clinging to his corkscrew curls.

After that summer, he disappeared
into Bloomington, Indiana.
We exchanged letters, one each, and stopped.

Sometimes I think of Guadalajara's
roses, its cantinas and fountains,
the squawk of macaws calling from the forest
where the bus released us further than we thought.

We found the wall where they jammed
Hidalgo's head on a stake,
three small, stiff squirrels lining the curb.

We found the mummies of Guanajuato
crowding a hill, babies in lace caps and trios of men,
teeth exposed to sing *rancheras* to themselves.

If I could wake you out of your heartland,
I would point my finger south,
toward a vanishing point of sand,
knowing full well:

When you placed that silver peso on the track,
to smear the face of a man
to alloy, entire histories disappeared.

The silver coin warms my palm,
the moment clear.

DENISE LEÓN
[ARGENTINA]

Denise León was born in Tucumán, Argentina, in 1974, granddaughter to Sephardic immigrants. She has published *Poemas de Estambul (Istambul Poems)*, (Alción, 2008), *El trayecto de la herida (Trajectory of the Wound)* (Alción, 2011), *El saco de Douglas (Douglas's Coat)* (Paradiso, 2011), *Templo de pescadores (Fishermen's Temple)*, (Alción, 2013), *Sala de espera (Waiting Room)* el CRUCEcartonero, 2013, and *Poemas de Middlebury (Middlebury Poems)* (Huesos de Jibia, 2014). She has participated in various international festivals including Rosario (2009), Córdoba (2014), Mendoza (2014), Festival Federal de la Palabra (2015) y Festival Internacional de Poesía de Buenos Aires (2015). Her poems have been included in various anthologies, including *Por mi boka (Through My Mouth)* (Lumen, 2013) and *Penúltimos (Penultimates). 33 poetas de Argentina 1965-1985 (33 Argentine Poets, 1965-|985)* (UNAM 2015), and translated to English and Portuguese. Among other distinctions, she has received Second Prize from Fondo Nacional de las Artes, Academia Argentina de Letras Prize and a 2011 Fulbrigth/ CONICET scholarship. She bears a Dotorate in Letters and is Joint Researcher at CONICET (Argentine Council for Scientific and Technical Research).

THE LIST

What he said.
What she said.
What his sister said,
his sister.
What they said,
those who saw them
go
and
come.
The old pertaining
to a group.
The trunk.
The source.
The same nobility
or
the same lowness.
Blood.
Water.
Again
water.
And
finally
she
who no longer listens.

LA LISTA

Lo que él dijo.
Lo que ella dijo.
Lo que dijo la hermana
de él.
Lo que dijeron
los que los vieron
ir
y
venir.
La vieja pertenencia
a un grupo.
El tronco.
La procedencia.
La misma nobleza
o
la misma bajeza.
La sangre.
El agua.
Otra vez
el agua.
Y
finalmente
ella
que ya no escucha.

JUANA M. RAMOS
[EL SALVADOR]

Juana M. Ramos was born in Santa Ana, El Salvador. She has been living in New York since 1990. She is a writer, poet and educator. As a poet she has participated and represented her country in different poetry conferences and cultural activities in New York City, México, El Salvador, Spain, Dominican Republic, Colombia, Honduras, Cuba, Argentina, and Puerto Rico. In June 2010 she published her first poetry book *Multiplicada en mí* and in 2014 a second edition revised and extended was published. Her poetry book *Palabras al borde de mis labios* was published in Mexico by miCieloediciones, 2015. Her poems have also appeared in anthologies, digital journals and blogs and literary magazines in Latin America and the United States.

HEREDERA

De mi padre heredé una especie de disgusto por la vida
y por los grupos de más de tres personas, la desconfianza
de los días calurosos que amagan lluvia, una aversión casi
completa a las visitas inesperadas, la taza de café y el cigarrillo,
la luz de su calle y la oscuridad de su casa,
el apego a la ausencia y la distancia.
Le debo a él frases cortas y largos hiatos,
la afición a las simples cosas,
el temblor recurrente en la mano derecha,
un desidioso paseo al río Anguiatú,
la marcha nupcial de Wagner,
la ineludible propensión al portazo y la huida,
un absurdo miedo a las mudanzas,
la hebra que a diario me remienda,
el "yo no como aquí",
su andar desordenado,
la cita quincenal eternamente trunca,
una biblia versión Reina Valera,
la pérdida, el desconsuelo,
la palabra alambicada, las hermanas que nunca conocí,
un par de tardes de danza en sus brazos,
su manera fronteriza de querer,
la herida en su costado,
el saludo reticente,
una sangre proclive a edulcorarse.
De mi padre lo heredé todo,
fobias, filias y sus periferias.
A mi padre lo heredé entero,
no sobró una astilla para mis hermanos.

JULIO MARZÁN
[PUERTO RICO]

poetryny.com
Julio Marzán —Puerto Rico—

Julio Marzán/J.A. Marzán, a graduate of Fordham U., (B.A.), Columbia U. (M.F.A), and New York U. (Ph.D.), was Poet Laureate of Queens, N.Y. from 2004-2007. Novel (as J.A. Marzán): *The Bonjour Gene*, University of Wisconsin Press' submission to the 2004 Pulitzer Prize: "Marzán displays the wit and intellectual verve rarely seen in contemporary literature.–Pulitzer Prize winner Oscar Hijuelos. Nonfiction: *The Spanish American Roots of William Carlos Williams*, (U. Texas Press): "Our gratitude will surely extend into the future beyond this magnificent book, …." Doris Sommer, Harvard University. Poetry: *Translations without Originals* (English) and *Puerta de Tierra* (Spanish). Poems in English appear in several editions of various college texts, among them *The Bedford Introduction to Literature*, *Latino Boom*, and *Literature: Reading to Write* and in distinguished journals, among them *Ploughshares, Tin House*, and *Harper's Magazine*. A profile of him was published in the fall 2009 issue of *Columbia Magazine*.

FOR DONALD TRUMP

> *Before I built a wall I'd ask to know*
> *What I was walling in or walling out.*
> —Robert Frost

"Let's raise this wall already there
up from its blueprint, the border,
too deep to dig under, so high
American stands insurmountable.

"Let's recite this wall to dam out
sludge of unforgiving history
brown as Mexicans pollute
a cleanly conquered continent.

"Let's recruit this wall to remember
our great waning enchantment
no ethnic readings should redact: *W
e want to be our beautiful story.*"

The story, of course, of this wall,
ink of settlement, slaughter, slavery
printed on pulp of white supremacy,
sanctimoniously bound in denial.

CARLOS SATIZÁBAL
[COLOMBIA]

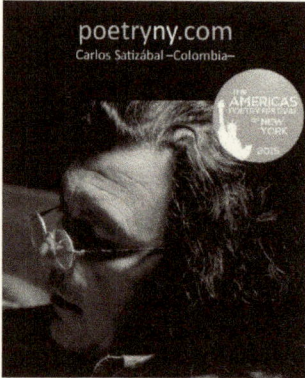

Carlos Satizábal was born in Palmira, Valle, Colombia, in 1959. A poet, actor, writer and director, he is Associate Professor at the National University of Colombia. He coordinates the Masters in Creative Writing Program and directs the course/playwriting workshop at the School of Film and TV. He studied Philosophy and Music at the Universidad del Valle. His book *The Flame Leaning* won the National Unpublished Poetry Prize in 2012. His work *They and Death – Dream of three poets* received the Playwriting Award Bogotá 2012. Satizábal works at Corporacion Colombiana de Teatro (CCT) as director, playwright, actor, composer and sound designer; with continuous processes of theatrical creation with displaced populations and victims of the war in Colombia. With Patricia Ariza, he founded Teatro Tramaluna more than 17 years ago. His work *Death or how to bury his father* has been published in the theatrical Anthology I by the National University of Colombia. One of his latest productions: *The Liberator: Love of Manuela and Simon* or *Dream of a Country not Founded*, premiered in Quito at the Bicentennial. His play *Rehearsal of Eternal Female Return*, received in Buenos Aires the 2015 Iberoamerican Playwriting Award Celcit 40 years.

WORD

Does perhaps the jaguar speaks to the lark?
Does the saman tree to the murmuring stones of the river bed
needs words to bury the roots and to drink the waters?

A very ancient or sacred law governs them.

Ah broken brain!
Within us... the Word.
She ordains the white certainty of death
And tell us to believe on the tiger's innocence that ignores it,
Eventhough is written in his blood and flesh.

Word that still does not understand the sing of the birds
ciphers in languages a paradise of deaths and passions.

In the middle of a cornfield the ringdoves fly
upon hearing the voices of harvesters that get nearby.

PALABRA

¿Habla acaso el jaguar con la alondra?
¿Acaso el samán con las rumorosas piedras del lecho
precisa de palabras para hundir sus raíces y beber las aguas?

Una ley antiquísima o divina les rige.

¡Ah roto cerebro!
En nosotros… la Palabra.
Ella ordena la blanca certeza de la muerte,
y nos dice creer en la inocencia del tigre que la ignora,
así esté escrito en su sangre y en su carne.

Palabra que aún sin comprender el canto de los pájaros
cifras en lenguajes un paraíso de muertes y pasiones.

En medio del maizal las torcazas alzan vuelo
al sentir la voz de los corteros que se acercan.

DANIEL BARUC
[DOMINICAN REPUBLIC]

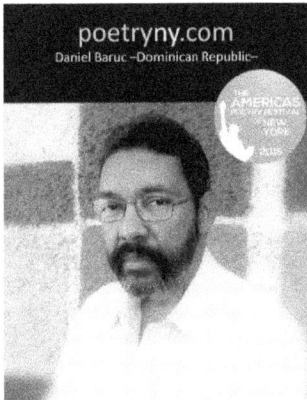

Daniel Baruc Espinal Rivera (Dominican Republic). Published works include: *Ceremonia en torno a una ausencia* (Santo Domingo, 2004), *Espejos del Sur* (Acapulco, 2005), *Piedad frutal* (Acapulco, 2006), *Cuentos para dormir demonios* (Acapulco, 2007), *Poner la mano en el fuego* (Puerto Rico, 2007), *Besar los ojos del fango* (Monterrey, 2010), *Roja iconografía de los otoños* (Nueva york, 2011), *La música y el vértigo* (Nueva York, 2013), *Máscaras, salamandras y unicornios* (Nueva York, 2014) and *Cuadernos del enjambre y del espejo* (México, 2015). Winner of the Premio Estatal de cuento "José Agustín" (Acapulco, 2007), Premio Estatal de Poesía "María Luisa Ocampo" (Acapulco, 2010), Premio Letras de Ultramar 2010 y 2012 (Nueva York), and third place in the Juegos Florales de la Plata (México, 2013). Honorable mention: Premio de Poesía "La puerta de los poetas" (París, 2007), Premio Mundial de poesía "Andrés Bello" (Venezuela, 2009), Premio de Poesía "Pedro Mir" (Santo Domingo, 2009), Premio de Poesía Copé Internacional (Perú, 2012) and IX Premio Bonaventuriano de Poesía (Colombia, 2013).

Voz de mar...

Voz de mar, en ti me reconozco húmedo de abismos.
Salitre fue la huella en el principio
y sol en las manos la búsqueda infinita.

La muerte, al fondo de las cerradas puertas, canta.
Sus manos grises huelen a naufragios y a cenizas.
¿Cómo se puede naufragar, pregunto,
cuando tus manos, tus ojos
y tus piernas están talladas de aguaceros?
¿Dónde dejará el viento los cartelones recios de su prisa
si el ocaso como un gran escarabajo rojo
ha ocupado la luz de tus pupilas?
¿Quién le tapará los ojos a la muerte? ¿Quién le cantará al oído?

EDGAR SMITH
[DOMINICAN REPUBLIC]

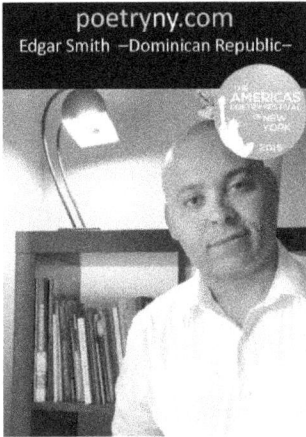

Edgar Smith, Dominican Republic, poet, translator, editor and writer, studied Marketing at UASD. Also studied English and German. Since the beginning of 2000, he has been posting poetry online, collaborating in various literary groups and blogs, besides administering his own blogs, El Palabrador and La Opinión Literaria. He has published two books of poetry, Algunas Tiernas Imprecisiones (A Few Tepid Misimpressions, 2013) and Island Boy (2014), a book of short stories, El Palabrador (The Wordsmith, 2013) and a novel, La Inmortalidad del Cangrejo (The Immortality of Crabs, 2015). Also in 2015, some of his poems have been included in the anthology, Solo para Locos Vol.2 (Just for the Crazy ones Vol.2). He has participated in several literary events: The 7th Hispanic/Latino Book Fair 2013, The 8th Dominican Book Fair 2014, The 8th Hispanic/Latino Book Fair 2014, The 1st Arts & Book Fair of Providence, the Voices of the Diaspora in NYC event 2014, the Censure those Lines event 2015, among others. Currently working on his third book of poetry, still untitled, and on his second book of short stories, *Weird Tales* (2016), as well as on his first English novel, *Gnuj & Alt*, and two more novels in Spanish, *La Pandemia* (The Pandemic) and *Arrimao* (Freeloading).

PARALLELISM

While I write
Someone agonizes
Someone plants gardenias
Someone unearths the bones of someone who wrote verses
Someone sees the moon
Someone (with a face, with a name, with a tear) rebuilds epochs on
the sand
And I, I carve holes in Time,
Thinking myself the epicenter
The sun of a galaxy that happens tied to my existence.
It eludes me that the others are suns to their own galaxies
Inexperienced gods with a quill and a gas lamp in their chests
predisposed to ceasing.
While someone writes with blood and sighs their unrepeatable story
I hesitate
I expire
I stop being.

PARALELISMO

Mientras yo escribo
alguien agoniza
alguien siembra gardenias
alguien desentierra huesos de alguien que escribía versos
alguien ve la luna
alguien (con un rostro, con un nombre, con una lágrima) restaura
épocas en la arena
y yo voy hollando el tiempo
creyéndome epicentro
sol de una galaxia que ocurre atada a mi existencia
me elude que los otros son soles de la suya
dioses inexpertos con una pluma y un candil en el pecho
predispuestos al cese.
Mientras alguien escribe con sangre y suspiros su historia irrepetible
yo vacilo
yo caduco
yo dejo de ser yo.

FRANCISCO ÁLVAREZ KOKI
[SPAIN]

poetryny.com
Francisco Álvarez Koki —Spain—

Francisco Álvarez Koki was born in A Guarda Galicia España in 1957. He has lived in NY since 1984. Koki is a bilingual autor (Gallego and Castilian). His most recent work in the Gallego language are: *Ratas en Manhattan*, (ediciones Sotelo Blanco, narrativa 2007), *Maruxia* (Diputación de Pontevedra, colección Cies 2010), *Un neno na emigracion* (edicions do cumio 2014). His recent work in Castilian include: *Ratas en Manhattan* (Chiado editora, Madrid 2013), *Entre tu cuerpo y mi cuerpo: antología amorosa del autor 1980 – 1996* (Diputación provincial de Pontevedra 2006), *Seis narradores españoles en NY* (ediciones Dauro Granada España 2006), *Piel palabra muestra de la poesía española en NY* (edición del Consulado general de España en Nueva York 2003), and *Al fin del siglo, 20 poetas antología de poetas hispanos en NY* (Ollantay press NY 2000).

SONATA TO A BODY BATHING IN A TUB

Like a vessel, the bathtub
Rocked you in time,
And I was your silence
Across the water.
Your exquisite body
Sank in the tenuous water,
While the moon fi ltered in
With all its mysteries.
The window blinds
Played with the wind,
And the tub embraced you
With its arms of iron.
The water forever
Climbed up your skin
With its tender swashing
To break your codes.
I was the gale
Stirring your sails,
I was the tsunami
Shaking your tub.
At the end, however, time was
Relentless, and I surrendered,
Becoming harbor and seashore,
To be the water in your bathtub.

SONATA PARA UN CUERPO EN LA BAÑERA

La bañera como un barco
te mecía en el tiempo,
y a través del agua
yo era tu silencio.
El agua tenue se hundía
por tu hermoso cuerpo
mientras la luna se filtraba
con todos sus misterios.
Los visillos de la ventana
jugaban con el viento,
mientras la bañera te rodeaba
con sus brazos de hierro.
El agua, otra vez el agua
en su dulce chapoteo
subía por tu piel
para entrar en tus secretos.
Yo era el vendaval
que soplaba en tus velas
y era el maremoto
que sacudía tu bañera.
Pero al final fue el tiempo
más firme que mi fuerza
y me volví playa y me volví puerto
para ser agua de tu misma bañera.

JORGE PAOLANTONIO
[ARGENTINA]

Jorge Paolantonio. Catamarca, Argentina, 1947. Poet, narrator, playwright. A professor of Anglo-Saxon language and literature. Theatre critic. He resides in Buenos Aires since 1981. Scholarship recipient: Fondo Nacional de las Artes; Council for the Arts (U. K.); ISA-Amsterdam.

He has published thirteen books of poems, most recently: *Baus* [2014] y *En este duro oficio* [anthology, 2015]. Paolantonio also has six published novels, most recently: *Traje de Lirio* [2014] y *Aguasanta* [2015]. In the theatre he has seventeen pieces compiled in four volumes, most recently: *Un dios menor* [2013].

Paolantonio has won a many awards including: Premio Nacional de Poesía (Zona NOA); First Place: 'Casa de Carriego'; 'Letras de Oro', Honorarte; First Place: Municipal de Novela de Buenos Aires; Internacional de Dramaturgia "Garzón Céspedes", Spain; *SoleLuna* de Novela, Italy; Nacional 'Esteban Echeverría'; Nacional de Cuento 'Micaela Bastidas'; from the brief novel 'Luis de Tejeda'. His work has been partially translated to English, Italian, Catalan, French, and Croatian.

corolla of (one's) existence
squatting there
stiff bas-reliefs
ourselves asking
why so many dogs
at the end of the night and if
those who loved us
will know where
our bones ended up
concealed for ever as they are
between manuscripts
and pins on the lips.

Translated from Spanish by Nora Isabel Degado

corola de la existencia
allí en cuclillas
bajorrelieves abarrotados
preguntándonos
porqué tantos perros
al final de la noche y si
aquellos que nos amaron
sabrán dónde
fueron a para nuestros huesos
disimulados para siempre
entre manuscritos
y alfileres en los labios.

Lena Retamoso
[Peru]

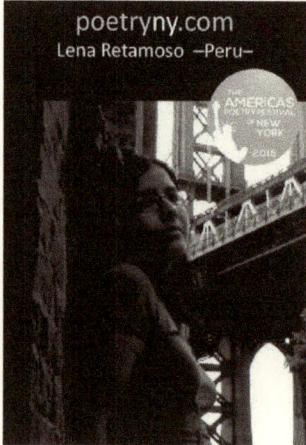

Lena Retamoso Urbano (Lima, 1978) is a P.H.D. candidate of Hispanic and Luso-Brasilian Literature at Graduate Center, CUNY, and is a teacher at City College, wherein she teaches Spanish and Hispanic Literature. She graduated from La Pontificia Universidad Católica del Perú (2002) and did her Master's degree at City College of New York (2006). She has published two poetry books: *Milagros de ausencia* (*Miracle of Absence*), 2002 and *Blanco es el sueño de la noche* (*White Is the Dream of the Night*), 2008.

my poem is weariness
weariness of being awake even in my deepest sleep
of dragging the days without feeling their weight or their beginning
of satiating hunger without time   without amazement
of thinking like someone who trains an infinite sequence of yawns
of giving voice to an ancient silence that only aspires to dilute
of making love feeling that love has come undone
and that you must coat again and again its prodigal membranes

my poem is weariness because my body is a word that no one exhumes
my word   a misplaced syllable in the jawbone of a fossil
my syllable   a well-spring of letters blind or groping
resting

scattering itself
on the invisible hearing
of a blank page

Translated from the Spanish by James J. Shay III

mi poema es cansancio
cansancio de estar despierto hasta en el sueño
de arrastrar los días sin sentirles el peso   ni el comienzo
de saciar el hambre sin tiempo   sin asombro
de pensar como quien entrena una secuencia infinita de bostezos
de darle voz a un silencio ancestral que solo aspira a diluirse
de hacer el amor sintiendo que el amor se deshizo
y hay que untarle una y otra vez sus pródigas membranas

mi poema es cansancio porque mi cuerpo es palabra que nadie exhuma
mi palabra   sílaba extraviada en la mandíbula de un fósil
mi sílaba   manantial de letras ciegas o a tientas
reposando

desparramándose

en los oídos invisibles
de una hoja en blanco

LILIA GUTIÉRREZ RIVEROS
[COLOMBIA]

Lilia Gutiérrez Riveros, Macaravita, Colombia. Poet, ensayist and narrator. Chemist, biologist and college professor. Poetry collections: *Con las alas del tiempo* (1985); *Carta para Nora Böring y otros poemas* (1994); *La cuarta hoja del trébol* (1997); *Intervalos* (2005); *Pasos alquilados* (2011)*; Inventarios* (2013); and *Sinfonía del Orbe, Poesía Completa*, Arte Poética Press, New York, 2014. Some of her poems have been translated into English, French, Portuguese, German, Italian and Chinese. Her work has been included in anthologies and critical studies. In 2010 she was awarded the first prize in the World Ecopoetry Contest. Gutiérrez Riveros is an Ambassador of peace from the universal Ambassadors of Peace Circle in Paris and Geneva. She is the founder and president of *Poesía sin fronteras*.

POCKET PLANET

I survey the lengthening of a sigh
And feel that we're entitled
To a world without garbage
Smokeless and deprived of weapons.

I feel the urge for a pocket planet
To stroll upon it barefoot
Unhurried and without schedules.

A planet with the smell of simple life
To plant embraces and utopias.

A planet to be shared
With trees and deer
Caterpillars, butterflies and dolphins
A planet with seas of medusas and crustaceans
And the migrations from arctic flights
As far as the Indian Ocean.

I survey the lengthening of a sigh
And protect inside the pocket
My planet of forests and mangrove swamps
Voiceless in the air, peaceful in the cities.

A planet whose people have green conscience
Their hands determined to improve life
And a soaring heart bursting by the edge of night.

Translated from the original in Spanish by Andres Berger Kiss

Planeta de bolsillo*

Recorro la elongación de un suspiro
y siento que tenemos derecho
a un mundo sin residuos
sin armas y sin humo.

Siento ganas de un planeta de bolsillo
para caminarlo a pie
sin prisa y sin horarios.

Un planeta con olor a vida simple
para sembrar abrazos y utopías.

Un planeta para respirarlo
con los árboles y los venados
orugas, mariposas y delfines.
Un planeta con mares de medusas y crustáceos
y la migración de vuelos del Ártico hasta el Índico.

Recorro la elongación de un suspiro
y protejo entre el bolsillo
mi planeta de bosques y manglares
sin ruidos en el aire y calma en las ciudades.

Un planeta con gente de conciencia verde
de manos dispuestas a madurar la vida
y el corazón crepitando al borde de la noche.

*Poema ganador del I CONCURSO MUNDIAL DE ECOPOESÍA, Tumbes, Perú, 2010

LINDA MORALES CABALLERO
[PERU]

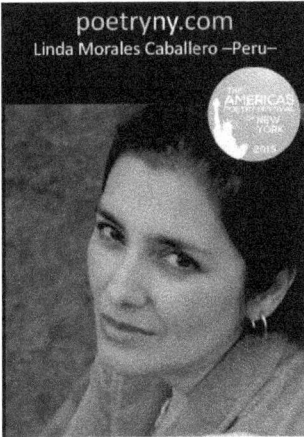

poetryny.com
Linda Morales Caballero –Peru–

Linda Morales Caballero was born in Peru, but has lived in several countries. She graduated Cum Laude from Hunter College she holds a Bachelor of Arts in Media Communications and Spanish Literature. Her Master's Degree is from the same institution. She has worked for CUNY, the Board of Education and the United Nations. Poetry books: *Desde el umbral (1989)*, *Circunferencia de la palabra* (1989), *The Edge of Twilight (1993)*, *Miradas de Nueva York (2000)*, *Poemas vivos: el Hombre adivinado, Poemas tuyos* (2005) *Encantamiento* (2013) *and Collage* (2014). Short stories: *El libro de los enigmas* (2014).

With LAIA, she created a yearly international literary contest and Anthology, and developed literary circles and creative writing workshops. Last year she co-founded the Literary Group: *Fuego de Luna*. Ms. Morales has been invited to readings and talks at Book Fairs and Festivals in New York, Buenos Aires, Brasilia, and Guadalajara.

Website: www.lindamoralescaballero.com

EVE

It was a moonlit night
inhabited by aquatic beings.

We swam against the current
tied by our hands
submerging in the bar
among mermaids.
Deep into the night,
among drunks.
Deep into time...
within the midnight prop craters.

Through the waves of the glances
I saw you passing through at once
by all perspectives...
from my stand point
I saw your insides...

And so I loved you,
but your confabulations started until
a dragon erupted from my mouth
the fire of a visceral and
well known rage.
My green desolation under the Manhattan planes
pierced you from my pupils.

I wished to tear you apart, and I did.
Suddenly, you became hair, saliva,
a diluted smile,
a distorted image.
The picture of the feared number...

The night ran like a river
to drain its tentacles at the sea
of the subconscious,
to reveal you that your icons
live in the hippocampus of my lost eyes...

You were so afraid about so much of so much in me…
that you madness turned into a scarecrow for children.
A game of chimneysweepers,
the organ grinder on the shadowed corner…
a life of invented nightmares.

Translated by Linda Morales, revised by Marko Miletich.

VÍSPERA

Fue una noche
lunar poblada de seres acuáticos.

Nadamos contra la corriente
atados de manos
bar adentro,
entre sirenas;
noche adentro,
entre beodos;
tiempo adentro…
en los cráteres de la utilería de las doce…

Por los oleajes de las miradas
te vi a la vez pasar por todas las perspectivas…
Desde mí, te vi por dentro…

Y así te amé,
pero confabulaste, hasta que
de mi boca eruptó un dragón
el fuego de una rabia visceral
y conocida,
mi verde desolación bajo los aviones
de Manhattan
te acribilló desde mis pupilas.

Tuve deseos de deshacerte, y lo hice.
De repente fuiste pelos, saliva,
sonrisa desleída,
la imagen distorsionada,
la foto del número temido…

La noche corrió como un río
a desaguar sus tentáculos en el mar
del inconsciente,
a revelarte que tus íconos
viven en el hipocampo de mis ojos perdidos…

Temiste tanto a tanto de tanto en mi…
que tu locura resultó tan sólo un espanto para niños,
un juego de deshollinadores,
el organillero de la esquina en penumbras…
una vida de inventadas pesadillas.

LUIS LUNA
[SPAIN]

poetryny.com
Luis Luna —Spain—

Luis Luna was born in Madrid, in 1975. PhD in Romanic Literature & BA in Hispanic Philology. He is a professor in UNED University and in Escuela de escritores (Creative Writing). He has published: *Notebook of the forester* (Amargord, 2007), *Al-Rihla* (Amargord, 2008), *Territory in semidarkness*, (Gens Ediciones, 2008), *Almond* (Amargord, 2010), *Umbilical* (El sastre de Apollinaire, 2012) and *Helor*. His complete work was published in EEUU as *Language rooms* by Artepoética Press.

FLAME'S LEARNING

It amazes you the heat, the uncertainty of the flame, the language of the smoke. Firelight proposes you/knowledges/that then don't forget. The tense dialog from the cold and the twilight with the bodies close to the light, impelled to it as the bird to the edge. It summoned not by the force of necessity nor the practice but also for the beauty. And the beauty also has the dark, what remains/writing in some way/ in the ash.

PEDAGOGÍA DE LA LLAMA

Te sorprende el calor, la incertidumbre de la llama, el lenguaje del humo. La lumbre te propone/aprendizajes/que luego no se olvidan. El diálogo tenso del frío y la penumbra con los cuerpos cercanos a la luz, impelidos a ella como el pájaro al canto. A ella convocados no por la fuerza de la necesidad ni la costumbre sino por la belleza. Y la belleza también posee lo oscuro, lo que queda/escrito de algún modo/ en la ceniza.

THROW THE STONE

at the pond's center
and you can not to see the circles.
What matters is the image that arises in your memory
the answer that vibrates in the empty hole of your hand

TIRAS LA PIEDRA

al centro del estanque
y no alcanza tu vista a ver los círculos.
Lo que importa es la imagen
que nace en tu memoria
la respuesta que vibra
en el hueco vacío de tu mano.

MARGARITA DRAGO
[ARGENTINA]

Margarita Drago is an Argentinean professor, poet and narrator who has lived in the USA since she was released from prison. As former political prisoner and writer she has participated in conferences, colloquia, book fairs and poetry festivals in the USA, Argentina, Peru, Brazil, Mexico, Honduras, El Salvador, Dominican Republic, Puerto Rico, Cuba, Spain and France. She is the author of the poetry collection *Con la memoria al ras de la garganta*; and the memoir *Fragmentos de la memoria. Recuerdos de una experiencia carcelaria (1975-1980)/ Memory Tracks. Fragments from Prison (1975-1980)*. Her work has appeared in literary and educational journals in the USA and Latin America.

HUBO UN TIEMPO

Hubo otoños y mañanas grises
y hojas secas en el patio
arremolinadas por el viento
hubo un parral generoso
cada octubre que prodigaba
sombra y frutos a sus dueños
hubo una casa asolada por las lluvias
invadida por la humedad y el miedo
hubo silencios que acuchillaban las gargantas
y llanto y clamor y gritos acumulados en el tiempo
hubo furia pasión rabia ira
y deseos muertos
y hubo dolor
mucho dolor empozado
en el alma y en los huesos
y hubo una mesa y un mantel y cuatro platos
y unas manos que cosían
y remendaban sábanas y recuerdos
y hubo un hombre
postrado ante una virgen
y una rosa   por la hija lejos
y una luz como una daga
que iluminó el silencio.

MARIANELA MEDRANO
[DOMINICAN REPUBLIC]

Marianela Medrano is a Dominican writer and poet, with a PhD in psychology living in Connecticut since 1990. Her individual publications include: *Oficio de Vivir* (Buho,1986), *Los Alegres Ojos de la Tristeza* (Buho,1987), *Regando Esencias/ The Scent of Waiting* (Alcance,1998), *Curada de Espantos* (Torremozas, 2002), *Diosas de la Yuca,* (Torremozas, 2011), Prietica (Alfaguara, 2013).

Medrano's work also appears in literary magazines and academic journals such as *Brooklyn Review* (1995), *Punto 7 Review* (1996) *Sisters of Caliban* (1996) *Callaloo* (2000), *Tertuliando/Hanging Out* (1997), *Letras Femeninas* (2005), *Kacike* (2009) *Trivia Voices of Feminism* (2009), *Journal of Poetry Therapy* (2010), *Sandplay Therapy Journal* (2010), *The Afro-Latin@ Reader* (2010), *Letralia* (2011), Phatitude (2012), Mujeres Como Islas II (2012), among others.

SORROWING

> *I will arise now, and go*
> *the city in the streets,*
> *and in the broad ways I will seek...*
> *whom my soul loves.*
> *Song of Songs 3:2*

Should I dye my hair red?
My old
old
old hair?
Red strands of curls to wrap
around his waist
and watch him gush forth dripping
birthing love again and again

Should I hang from his hands like a kite
soaring or sorrowing   all in red?
I have no fear of love
of soaking in the viscosity
of a deferred dream
that strips me of my name
Nameless I wander the streets
dismantled

My fingers swirl corpses—strand by strand
So many have died in Gaza
Six-year-old Mohamed startles me
a three-inch-long gash in his torso
I stop wandering the wintry morning
to smear red over his brown body—
An aching memory
his pain revives my own
I wait—standing still in the palette of sorrow
gesture to light a cigarette
then remember I don't smoke

Warily I smile to an old woman
pilfering hearts on the streets

Should I dye my hair red
to dispel the voice no longer calling me?
Should I wake up to darkness soaring like a kite in his hands?
Hands of the lover—that is
I start off again
chanting news of broken hearts from Gaza's
to my own—then decide   red looks good
looks good It looks really good.

PENANDO

> *I will arise now, and go*
> *about the city in the streets,*
> *and in the broad ways I will seek...*
> *whom my soul loves.*
> *Song of Songs 3:2*

¿Debería teñirme el pelo de rojo?
¿Mi pelo viejo
muy viejo?
Mechones rizos que amarro
a su cintura
y le miro lanzarse hacia adelante goteando
Dando a luz al amor una y otra vez

¿Debería colgar de sus manos como una cometa
volando o penando toda roja?
No le tengo miedo al amor
A empaparme en la
viscosidad de un sueño deferido
que se roba mi nombre

Sin nombre deambulo las calles
Desmantelada

Mis dedos viran cadáveres—hebra a hebra
Tantos han muerto en Gaza
Mohamed—con apenas seís años me espanta
Una herida de tres pulgadas en su torso
Dejo de deambular en la mañana invernal
para untar rojo en su cuerpo marrón—memoria doliente
su dolor revive el mío

Espero—parada quietamente en la paleta de la pena
Gesticulo y enciendo un cigarrillo
entonces me acuerdo que no fumo
Cansada sonrío a una mujer
que roba corazones en la calle

¿Debería teñirme el pelo de rojo
para disipar la voz que no me llama más?
¿Debería despertar a la oscuridad volando como cometa en sus
manos?
Manos del amante—quiero decir
Salgo de nuevo
Cantando noticias de corazones rotos desde el de Gaza hasta el mío—
entonces decido
que el rojo se ve bien
Se ve muy bien.

MARINA OROZA
[SPAIN]

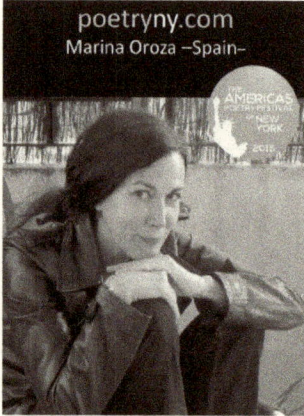

Marina Oroza is a Spanish poet and writer who has also succeeded in the world of artistic performance and acting. She has participated in festivals, theaters, universities, foundations, and museums in Spain, France, Ireland, and Portugal. She also collaborates with visual artists and musicians. Oroza has published the following books of poems: *La Chimenea de Duchamp* (Ardora 2014), *Así quiero morir un día* (Huerga y Fierro 2005) and *Pulso de Vientos*, illustrated by Juan Genovés with a text by Jesús Ferrero (Ketres 1997). Some of her work has been included in national and international anthologies such as *Poetas en Blanco y Negro* (Abada 2006), and editorials in magazines and press. She collaborates in an online radio (elestadomental.com). She also edited a DVD of the performance repertoire Disección poética en público (2006) and a CD of the concert repertoire Mirabilia (2004). Some of her poems have been translated to Catalan and English. www.marinaoroza.com

AURA

In reality that corner
is a quagmire of reincarnations
converted into mourning shrouds.
In reality the shape of things
is a palpable aura,
a soul, a hollow eclipse,
a waterfall of frozen horizon
with nothing to hide.
In reality, the skin of the morning
is the same as the night's,
physically emptied island.
We are air fossil
and we are there, that's all,
like the shape of things,
like noblemen without their slaves
and then we invent symbols
that are vessels so we can
finally name what does not exist.

AURA

En realidad esta esquina
es un lodazal de reencarnaciones
convertidas en fundas de luto.
En realidad la forma de las cosas
es un aura palpable,
un alma, un eclipse hueco,
una cascada de horizonte helado
sin nada que ocultar.
En realidad la piel de la mañana
es la misma que la piel de la noche,
físicamente isla vaciada.
Somos fósil de aire
y estamos ahí, sin más,
como la forma de las cosas,
como nobles sin esclavos
y entonces inventamos símbolos
que son cuerpos para poder
nombrar de una vez lo que existe.

Marta López-Luaces
[Spain]

poetryny.com
Marta López-Luaces –Spain–

Marta López-Luaces was born in Galicia, Spain, in 1964. She is a poet, writer, and translator. She holds a Ph. D. in Spanish and Latin American Literatures from New York University (2000). As a poet, she has published the collections, *Distancias y destierros* (Sgo. de Chile, 1998), *Las lenguas del viajero* (Madrid, 2005) and *Los arquitectos de lo imaginario* (Valencia, Spain, 2011) and the chapbook, *Memorias de un vacío* (New York, 2000). In 2011, her book *Los arquitectos de lo imaginario* was finalist of the prestigious award Ausias March. This collection has been recently translated into English by G. J. Rackz. Her poetry in English was published in the prestigious literary journal *Confrotation, The Hampden-Sydney Poetry Review, Sakura Review, downtown brooklyn, Literary Review* y *Mandorla* Her poetry has been translated into English, Romanian, Italian and Portuguese, and published in literary journals and anthologies in Latin America, Europe, and the United States. She published the collection of short stories *La Virgen de la Noche* (Madrid: Sial, 2009) and the novel, *Los traductores del viento* (Madrid-Monterrey: Vaso Roto, 2013). *Los traductores del viento* had excellent reviews and won the Internal Latino Book Award 2014.

DIANA

Against your nature
the solitude you believe in.

Within you is an uninhabited
plague
that sorrow translates as distance.

Return to your mountains
recovered
by origins
and by abysses.

Against your nature
the wrath that spreads
through the soul's lineage.

Arrive
with pride at your failures.

Tanslated from Spanish by Juan Manuel López Ramos

DIANA

En contra de tu ser
la soledad en que crees

Todo en ti deshabitada
peste
que la nostalgia traduce en distancia

Regresa a tus montañas
recobrada
de origen
y de abismo
En tu contra
la cólera que se propaga
por el linaje del alma

Llega
erguida a tu falta

Matías Escalera Cordero
[Spain]

Matías Escalera Cordero was born in Madrid in 1956. He is the author of the novels *Un mar invisible* (2009), *El tiempo cifrado* (2014), and of the collection of short stories *Historias de este mundo* (2011). He has also written poetry: *Grito y realidad* (2008), *Pero no islas* (2009) and *Versos de invierno: para un verano sin fin* (2014). As a playwright, he wrote *El refugio* (awarded in 2009). His works has been included in several Anthologies and collective books as we can see in *Por donde pasa la poesía* (2012), *En legítima defensa: poetas en tiempos de crisis* (2014), *Disidentes* (2015). He witnessed the end of The Cold War while working as a Spanish and Literature teacher first in Moscow and later in Ljubljana –capital of Slovenia– former Yugoslavian Republic. He has been collaborating with some International magazines and his critical profile appears for instance in the book *La (re)conquista de la realidad* (2007) of which he is coordinator, and in the collective book *La República y la cultura. Paz, guerra y exilio* (2009). He is director of the online magazine *Youkali* (www.youkali.net) and member of the board of the International editorial team of the Hispanic Philology magazine *Verba Hispanica* at Ljubljana University in which he worked as a lecturer.

ONE HUNDRED TIMES DEAD (EACH DAY)

Today I have died one hundred times on the bridges...
(perhaps you don't understand it?) One hundred times on
And one hundred times below the bridges...

One hundred times on the street...
and one hundred times below the street...

Today (or maybe it was yesterday
and before yesterday as well) I have been displaced
Thrown out received released thrashed hung torn out...

I have died one hundred times (as a dog dies) one hundred times
On the street
And one hundred times below the street...
On the bridges and under the bridges (don't speak to me
about the last payment
nor of our kids: nor of their dreams...) Be silent
Come: simply come close and lay at my side...

And caress me while I sleep...

...

Of the tiredness light is born
In the darkness I return to you (without dreams)

Translated from Spanish by Zachary Payne

CIEN VECES MUERTO (CADA DÍA)

Hoy he muerto cien veces encima de los puentes...
(¿acaso no lo entiendes?) Cien veces encima
Y cien veces debajo de los puentes...

Cien veces encima del asfalto...
Y cien veces debajo del asfalto...

Hoy (o tal vez fue ayer
y antes de ayer también) He sido desplazado
Arrojado recibido despedido vapuleado colgado arrancado...

He muerto cien veces (como muere un perro) Cien veces
Sobre el asfalto
Y cien veces debajo del asfalto...

Sobre los puentes y bajo los puentes (no me hables
del último plazo
ni de nuestros hijos: tampoco de tus sueños...) Calla
Ven: sólo acércate y acuéstate a mi lado...

Y acaríciame mientras duermo...

...

Del cansancio nace la luz
En la oscuridad vuelvo a ti (sin sueños)

MAUREEN H. ALTMAN
[USA/PERU]

poetryny.com
Maureen H. Altman –USA/Peru–

Maureen H. Altman was born in Georgia, U.S.A. and was raised in Lima, Peru. She was accepted at The National Peruvian School of Fine Arts, where she studied drawing and painting. She obtained a Bachellor Degree in Fine Arts at Pratt Institute, New York, and graduated with a Master of Science in regular-special education at Touro College, New York. Altman is an autodidact in poetry. *Encuentro, amor, vida, tiempo…* is her first poetry book, published by Urpi Editors in 2014. *Matices* is her second poetry book, published in 2015 by La Ovejita Books. Both books were printed in New York. As an artist, Altman recently participated in group exhibitions in Lima and Rio de Janeiro. Currently, she directs Educa.Arts, program designed to educate through art, poetry and creative writing. Also, she directs Altman Art Studio, atelier which developed the First Annual Salon in August 2014.

YOUR EYES

Your eyes like breeze,
lay crossing the road
from the path of truth
calling the morning
for its glance...

Eyes covering, eyes on hold,
eyes shocking, eyes at the end sign
telling more than can be seeing
and your eyes,
are not gone...

I look with closed eyes
at the station, at the wild,
at the Ferris wheel, at times,
your time is due, maybe,
and my eyes reopen...

Destiny, who can see you?
a chance, a moment,
an open mind,
endurance, acceptance
staying still...

My eyes stay on those landscapes
and the road closes them
so airily,
your eyes are seeing
our passage forever...

MICHELE KARAS
[USA]

A native San Diegan, Michele Karas works as an associate copy director for a top-five U.S. book publisher and studies poetry in the MFA program at the City College of New York, where she is also a graduate editor for the *Promethean Literary Journal*. Her poems and essays have appeared or are forthcoming in *Narrative, Thrush Poetry Journal, Pea River Journal*, and *Alaska Quarterly Review*, among other publications. Find her on Twitter @ small_peace.

DROWN

A curly worm sheathed
in a miniature coat of armor.
The rattle of a metal
gate being drawn.

I never told anyone about
the summer I dropped
that pill bug
into the gutter
in front of our house.

Angry little fist,
inert little insect
curled in on itself.

It was like a silver bullet,
furious in its downward spiral.

How does a life get to be so small?

The clarity of the memory
alternates between murky,
sharp, impossible to see
the truth, the depth too
unfathomable.

MICHELLE YASMINE VALLADARES
[INDIA/KUWAIT/USA-]

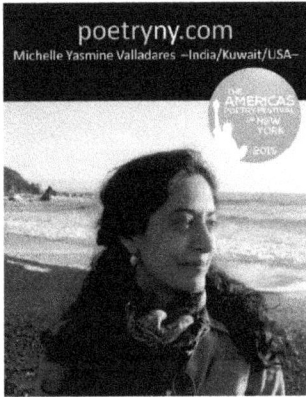

Michelle Yasmine Valladares is a poet and film producer, born in India, raised in Kuwait and currently resides in the US. She is the author of *Nortada, The North Wind* (Global City Press). Her poem "Papers and Pearls" was nominated for a Pushcart Prize in 2014. Her publications include *Clockhouse, The Literary Review* and the anthologies, *Language for a New Century: Contemporary Poetry from the Middle East, Asia & Beyond*, and *The HarperCollins Book of English Poetry by Indians*. She co-produced the Brazilian film, *O Sertão das Memórias,* directed by José Araújo which won *Best Latin American Film, 1997 Sundance Film Festival* and the *Wolfgang Staudte Prize* at the Berlin Film Festival. She co-produced *El Diablo Nunca Duerme* directed by Lourdes Portillo in Mexico/US and worked with Hopi filmmaker, Victor Masayesva, Jr. on his documentary, *Imagining Indians.* She is the MFA Lecturer in Poetry at The City College of New York.

The Book of Trees

How to tell chestnut from sycamore
or rowan from beech or fir?
Walking with my head buried in the book of trees, I fail
the test of cluster of five leaves,
mottled edge, berries or long pod.
The Scots have river, firth,
burn, loch and sea.

I know Sahara and Sonora,
the desert dust and storm,
the Atlantic swells and Pacific's
crashing surf. I learned to swim
in the shallows of the Arabian Gulf,
spent summers near the Indian Ocean.

In the cool air and light of a Scottish
trail, I hear my father-in-law's voice,
copper beech, chestnut and lime,
a river running backwards, a yew
tree older than the churchyard.
Is it memory that we gain
or remembering what we once
knew whispered, before the fairy
tale and childhood rhyme?

MIGUEL FALQUEZ-CERTAIN
[COLOMBIA/USA]

poetryny.com
Miguel Falquez-Certain –Colombia/USA–

Miguel Falquez-Certain (Barranquilla, Colombia) has been living in New York City for four decades, where he works as a multilingual translator and writer. He is the author of six volumes of poetry: Reflejos de una máscara, Habitación en la palabra, Proemas en cámara ardiente, Doble corona, Usurpaciones y deicidios, and Palimpsestos; of a short novel, Bajo el adoquín, la playa; of six plays: La pasión, Moves Meet Metes Move: A Tragic Farce, "Castillos de arena," "Allá en el club hay un runrún," "Una angustia se abre paso entre los huesos," and Quemar las naves, as well as of short stories and essays. Book Press–New York published Triacas (short fiction) and Mañanayer (poetry) in 2010. Mañanayer received the only honorable mention in The 2011 International Latino Book Awards in the category of Best Poetry Book – Spanish or Bilingual. He has participated in book fairs in Miami, Santo Domingo, New York, and Bogotá, and he has been a guest poet at literary conferences and festivals in Ecuador and the U.S.A. He translated both screenplays for Steven Soderbergh's Che Guevara biopics, The Argentine and Guerrilla. He is a member of PEN American Center, The American Translators Association, and Proz.com.

GIFT

Rhythmically, the sun kisses
In quick waves, estuary
Overflowing your waist,
Sweet, feverish path
Traversed in secrecy,
Biting ecstasy, mine...
Your lethargic flavor,
Undergrowth you're offering me
Among the trills, sparkles
Fastening you to the molds
Finally choking off your dare.

In the undergrowth, your generous
Gift makes me fertile.

DÁDIVA

El sol besa cadencioso
en rápido ondular, ría
que desborda tu cintura,
febril y dulce camino
recorrido con sigilo,
éxtasis mordiente, mío
tu sabor aletargado,
espesura que me brindas
en los trinos, las centellas
que te fijan en los moldes
truncando ya el desafío.

Tu generosa dádiva
en la espesura me fecunda.

MIRIAM MEJÍA
[DOMINICAN REPUBLIC]

poetryny.com
Miriam Mejía –Dominican Republic–

Miriam Mejía is a Dominican writer and a resident of New York. She studied statistics and sociology in the Universidad Autonoma of Santo Domingo. She has written: "*Crisálida*" (stories, 1997); "*De Fantasmas interiores y otras complejidades*" (stories, 2004); "*Garabatos en púrpura*" (essays and stories, 2007); "*Piel de agua*" (poetry, 2008); "*Aristas ancestrales*" (poetry, 2010); "*Mujeres en claves*" (2010). She co-write: "*El final del silencio*" (poetry, 2009); "*Pincelando las palabras*" (poetry, 2010), "*El danzar de las palabras*" (poetry, 2011); "La *palabra rebelada/revelada: el poder de contarnos*" (2011) and "...*y la imagen se hizo verso*" (2012). Her work appears in the following anthologies: *Di aroma di café* (2006); *Antología de cuentistas dominicanas* (2007); *Voces de la Inmigración* (2007): *Gente de pocas palabras* (2014), *Donde dije digo* (2014), *Mirada de haijin* (2015), *Confesión de partes, aforismos y fragmentos* (2015), *Para no cansarles con el cuento* (2015) and *A la cuenta de tres, microcuentos* (2015).

AMIGA

Mujer amiga,
eres trillo zigzagueante
entre hierbas estremecidas de rocío,
brisa que retoza juguetona
sobre la piel del viejo río.
Mujer hermana,
silabario no escrito,
re-juego de palabras reinventadas
en un instante
de dolorosa tensión,
amor de cuna,
pasión adulta,
ruego quedo,
quejido roto,
deslizándose a tientas
y en soledad trémula,
por el silencio tímido
de una habitación.
Cadencia de un poema,
cantando a la salud y la sabiduría,
canción de arpegios púrpura
en rítmico nacimiento,
desde las profundidades
del cristal ambarino de un diapasón.
Noche, alba, día en sincrónica trilogía.
Eres enojo liviano,
llanto y congojas compartidos.
Lluvia mustia, granizo rojo,
te de bayahonda y cadillo.
Emplasto de guazábara,
caricia de áloe,
jabón de cuaba,
infusión de tilo,
friega y sahumerio
en reposo bendecido.
Respiración sosegada,

recostada en la madrugada,
convocatoria silente
de exorcismo cotidiano.
Mujeramigahermana,
te admiro en tu quehacer,
todo fluye, todo queda,
no estas sola.
Nos une un brindis vigoroso,
en copas de cristal,
rebosantes de miel,
templadas en la fragua
de la esperanza
y al amparo de solidaridades
anaranjadas de un atardecer.

MONICA CARRILLO ZEGARRA
[PERU]

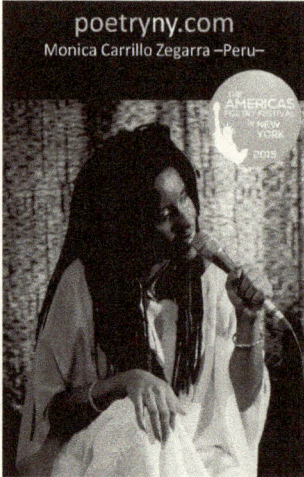

Monica Carrillo Zegarra (MFA´s candidate Performance Interactive & Media Arts , CUNY/Brooklyn College), an Afro-Peruvian writer, poet, singer, musician, community leader, journalist, human rights advocate, and feminist working with her organization LUNDU Center for Afro Peruvian Studies and Advancement . Carrillo, who goes by the name Oru, creates poetry that mixes afro-beat, hip-hop and Afro Peruvian music to bring attention to the ongoing effects of racism and sexism. Her production "Unicroma" included a CD, a book and a performance with 8 musicians and dancers and has been featured on MTV Europe. Her poetry was translated in Catalan and German and it is a subject of academic studies by universities of Italy, Chile, Argentina y Peru and the European Union. She rang the Bell in NASDAQ in the International Women Rights Day (2007) and she was a keynoter with the Hollywood's actor Richard Gere in the Gala "Invest in Women" hosted by IWHC. She has given conferences in Harvard, Columbia and around the globe. Carrillo is the recipient of the recognition of Google in the "Human Map" and she is in the category "Peru" in The Google Earth Map. She was the image of the campaign "Every Human Has Rights" of the organization The Elders, founded by Nelson Mandela and Desmond Tutu and Carrillo was honored by Rutgers University with 16 women around the world who standout in the fight against gender violence. Her work was featured in PBS, Univision, Aljazeera, BBC.

Photo by Tammy Dobson.

A Cimarrona's Runner (A Runaway Maroon)

Run, jump, scratch
You got to the mountain
You swam the river
The green of the
Pajaro Bobo
Envelopes you
There's no jungle here
As in Palmares
Nor the rivers
Of Esmeralda
Here the pampas
Sticks the dust
In your nose…

Where should I go if there's a mountain range
Or a horizon that discovers me?

I trust and pray
I drill the hill
Make up a haven
But don't come back
I first assault
Scare or murder
Eat up my crap
And am well fed.

The hound barks
Smells my steps
I can't even
Retain my breath
I leave it all
Right in the way
So that when it
Bites at my haunch
It can't pick out
My slave body

'Cause if I die
Between its teeth
I will die free
Not "freed slave"
Thanks to some mercy.

He already fled
Without return
Perhaps he awaits me
And dreams of seeing me,

(Maybe the leg
The hound fetched
Back to the farm
Wasn't his leg)

Maybe destiny
Will come with us,
The hound barks
There's no jungle here
The hill is low
I reached a river
That's seaward bound...

I can't go on!
I can't go on!!!
Too many days
And there's no strength,
My sweet Orula ...
Why do you take me
So hopelessly?
Is there no solace
In this life?
I see the sky
Tormented
By my departure.

(Oru Orula
Oru Oru Orula
Don't be cruel

Caress her
Orula
Don't be cruel
Orula…)

There's a cliff
And I slide down
Knead the mud
While I crawl
There's no more silence
I hear chants…
Hope comes back
I can see fire…

It's a palenque
Receiving me
And there he is,
There's a gap
Below his knees

(The leg the dog
Snatched away)

But he's always waiting
For me on his feet
Just like the trees
Just like a warrior
Under a mask
Of tree trunk made.

Now I'm not alone,
Now I'm not alone,
I've got my axé

NANCY MERCADO
[USA/PUERTO RICO]

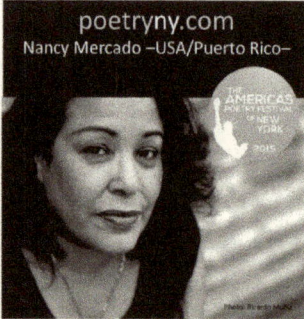

Nancy Mercado is the editor of the Nuyorican Women Writers Anthology published in Voices e/Magazine: a City University of New York online literary journal. Featured on National Public Radio and on the PBS NewsHour Special: America Remembers 9/11, her work is extensively anthologized internationally. Recently, She traveled to Havana, Cuba, by invitation, where she presented her work in Casa de las Americas. She is currently a guest curator for the Museum of American Poetics and assistant editor of Eco-Poetry.org. Nancy is the author of It Concerns the Madness (Long Shot Productions). For more information, please go to: http://www.nancy-mercado.com

SILENCE

Who could detain me with useless illusions
when my soul begins to complete its work
—Julia De Burgos

When the joker appears
With mouthfuls of shadows and smoke
Crazily waving his self-import in my face
Like flags waving front suburban homes
As if to cover the hate crimes of this country

When he yells to idle my mind
Spewing out vortexes in tongues
Filled with false virtues
Like commercials that mask
The plunder of impoverished lives
The enslavement of darker skin
The raping of female years
I know the joker is oblivious
That his time steadily dwindles
Like any man's life
That a pine box
A crematorium await him
Just as they await me
That he does not know
My silence is an impenetrable shield

SILENCIO

¿Quién podrá detenerme con ensueños inútiles
cuando mi alma comience a cumplir su tarea?
—Julia de Burgos

Cuando el burlón aparezca
Con bocados de sombras y humo
Hondeando agitadamente su altanera
En mi cara
Cual bandera flotante al viento
Frente a las villas de los suburbios
Como para encubrir los crímenes de esta nación

Cuando vocifera para neutralizar mi pensamiento
Escupiendo torbellinos en mensajes
Preñados de falsos valores
Cual anuncios que desfiguran
El saqueo de las vidas empobrecidas
La esclavitud de la piel oscura
Las violaciones de los anos femeninos,
Yo sé que el burlón esta ajeno
Al tiempo que lentamente se desvanece así
Como la vida de cualquiera
En una caja de pino
Camino del crematorio
Como me aguarda a mí
Sin que él se dé cuenta
Que mi silencio
Es una coraza impenetrable

Traducción del Inglés por Alejandro Villalba

TONIA LEON
[USA]

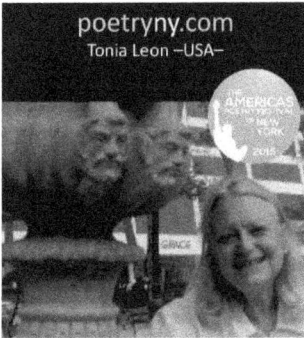

Born in Brooklyn, Tonia Leon has written poetry since she was a child. Her poetry, prose and in English as well as Spanish has been published here and abroad. Her poetry reflects her passions: ecology, trees, music, Mexico, and social justice to name just a few. She is currently working on a second chapbook and translations of poetry from Spanish to English. Tonia lives on Long Island.

LEAVING THE TOWN OF BENITO JUAREZ

I say goodbye to the green humming birds
and the little blue lizards
they're not to be found in New York
and if they had once resided here
we would have finished them off long ago
burying them beneath these sidewalks of cement.

SALIDA DEL MUNICIPIO DE BENITO JUÁREZ

Me despido de las chuparrosas verdes
y las lagartijas azules.
No existen en Nueva York.
Y si hubiesen existido
hacía tiempo que
las hubiéramos acabado
enterradas bajo las aceras de cement.

Norma Feliz Peralta
[Dominican Republic]

Norma Feliz Peralta was born in Constanza, Dominican Republic and has lived in New York City since 1989. Norma has degrees from Hostos Community College in Public Administration (1998), Lehman College in Therapeutic Recreation (2003). Currently, she studies Spanish Literature in The City College of New York. Her published books are: *Madrugadas* (2008), *La Muralla* (2009), *Cipango* (2010) a shared book with Dr. Martha Crosby (2012), *Poemas de familia* (2012), and *Wii-ken* (2014).

Lindero Eter-no

A todos nos amamanta el tiempo. El abrigo de la muerte. La efeméride del amor. Salón eterno experimenta mudas. Y el teatro desaparece versos verdaderos. Nadie escucha. Sólo existo en la intimidad de la virtud, en la taza de café que traga mi boca atiborrada de tiempo, sábanas manchadas de versos...

Abanico abierto. Animado. Despuntando letras encima de mi sexo. Palabras quebrantan ventanas, libros y puertas penetradas por solemnes huidas.

Este movimiento oscuro entre manos transparentes...atado por el minúsculo silencio. Gime el presente. Árbol de invenciones. Esperanza. Neblinas de incendios hunden el infinito en átomos de tiempo. Y agudiza.

A todos nos amamanta el tiempo. Plumas y taparrabos los hemos sacado para ser objetos, orgullos. Diferencia entre primaveras y soles... que se esconden tras frases bien dichas

PATRICIA ARIZA
[COLOMBIA]

Patricia Ariza is a poet, playwright, direc-tor, stage designer and social and feminist activist. During her youth she took part in the *Nadaismo* movement. In 1966, she and Santiago García founded the culture house Teatro La Candelaria. This was the first alternative theater in Colombia. She was founded whit Santiago García, Enrique Buenaventura, and others, the Colombian Theater Organization: Cor-poración Colombiana de Teatro. From 1967 to 1969 she studied Art History at the National University of Colombia in Bogota. Ariza distinguishes herself in the theatrical world for her special approach which focuses on promoting social interaction and reducing conflicts. In 2007 she was honored with a Culture and conflict Prince Claus Award from the Netherlands. Her book *Hojas de papel volando*, received a National poetry award in Colombia. In 2014, she received The Gilder/Coigney International Theatre Award.

MY HOUSE

There's only a small
house, the original one,
and it's on a corner.
Inside, some gestures remain
which I go over in minute detail.
On the second floor
is the manner, intact,
in which my father grasped
a hammer.
Closer, in the kitchen
the grace with which
my mother cut
onions.
In the dining room and
on the staircase
the nighttime footsteps of my uncle
who was crazy.
Close to my bed
the key to the trunk
which held my sister's
folded dresses.
And in the windowpane,
even now, the eyes of a
girl with the fear
of leaving.

Translated from Spanish by Alice Emery

MI CASA

Sólo hay una casa
Pequeña, primigenia
Y queda en una esquina.

Allí dentro, reposan todavía
algunos gestos que recorro minuciosamente.
En el segundo piso
está intacto el modo
de mi padre empuñar
el martillo.

Más cerca, en la cocina
la gracia con que
mi mamá picaba
la cebolla.

En el comedor y
la escalera
los pasos en la noche
de mi tío que estaba loco.

Cerca de mi cama
la llave del baúl que
guardaba los vestidos
doblados de mi Hermana.

Y en el vidrio de la
ventana, los ojos de una
niña con el miedo intacto
de salir.

ROBERTO FERNÁNDEZ-IGLESIAS
[MEXICO/PANAMA]

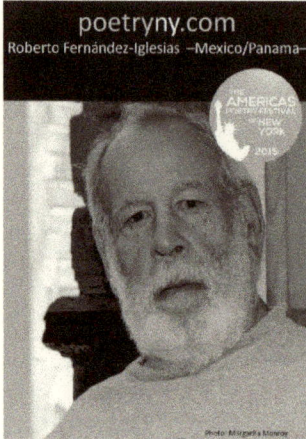

poetryny.com
Roberto Fernández-Iglesias –Mexico/Panama–

Roberto Fernández-Iglesias.- Mexican; born in Panama (1941). BA in Philosophy and Literature, University of Panama,1970; graduate studies in Ibero-American Literature and Communication Science, UNAM, Mexico. Retired professor of the University of the State of Mexico. Retired professor, School of Social and Political Sciences, UNAM. Professor of the Writer's School (SOGEM) – Cuernavaca, Morelos and of the Writer's School of Metepec, State of Mexico. Between 1957 and 1966, editor of 80 editions of the first stage of the literary magazine *tunAstral*. Editor, between the years of 1966 and 1972, in Panama of the magazine *Participation – Poetry* and the books Participation. Back in Mexico in 1972, coordinated the collection "Abra Palabra" and the "Pablo Neruda Literary Workshop" from the government of the State of Mexico, which continued until the 80's. Published the following books: *Recits*; *Canciones retorcidas* (The Ricardo Miró National Poetry Prize,1973);Soñar tu sombra; *El gran desnudo y Primer Placer*; *Dieciocho narraciones breves*; *Celebrar la palabra*; *Retrato parcial*; *Trastienda*; *Falso contacto*; *En tiempo de recuerdo*; *Furiosa sustancia*; *Poemas juntos y revueltos*; Canciones retorcidas, Resorte y otras formas (poems, Arte Poética Press, New York, USA, 2015). Director/Founder *tunAstral* and *cAmbiAvíA*.

In some far-off place
as happens
in every story
worthy
    of
        the telling
they have erected
a monument

to memory
and they build it
with fragile stone
to be able to destroy
it

each

day

 The many-petaled
flower
sleeps on the air
and stirs
We many petals
as we stir
when
     the
        air

changes
       we
fall

He felt strong
emaciatedly solid
until it happened:
that
    long
        instant
of the breaking off
of the first leaf

that

is still
falling

You saw her growing
and she was always
growing
It seems that when
her growing stopped
you stopped seeing

There are afternoons
spent drinking coffee
thinking
        and on
one of them
You write a poem
        and on another
you talk
        and
there are more afternoons

Translated from Spanish by Donald Walsh

ROSSALINNA BENJAMIN
[DOMINICAN REPUBLIC]

Rossalinna Benjamin, Dominican Republic, 1979. Poet and educator. Education: Education Mention Spanish Language Studies, O&M Dominican University, Specialist in Culture and Spanish Language, International Iberoamerican University (UNINI) *Books*: "Manual to assassinate narcissi", "diary of the detachment" (Poetry). *Awards*: Honorable Mention Category University, National Contest of Literary's Workshops Santo Domingo 2008 -National Youth Poetry Award International Book Fair Santo Domingo 2011, Particular Mention Nosside World Poetry Award Italy 2014.

ESCENARIO

Al mismo tiempo que la rabia
te da una mordida estratégica en el último esfínter,
el dolor te introduce su lengua salada en los oídos,
cada cual más pavorosamente seductor
y tú pierdes la capacidad de decidir,
porque una niña rota se acurruca en el lugar
donde debería estar el rayo
que mueve tu índice hacia el frente.

No quedan más que dudas en harapos,
suspiros chamuscados esparcidos por la estancia,
manos muertas sobre el teclado,
señales de STOP enmarañadas
entre el deseo descompuesto
y la frescura del hastío.

El aaaaahhhh!! repetido por cada hilo estrangulado,
mientras te cosen y tallan y tejen y te reinventan,
infinitamente desfigurada,
en los vestidos ajenos al papel
que hoy ensaya tu osamenta,
revolcándose en la alfombra
y el telón que nunca cierra.

Viene bien el auditorio de repente desierto,
la furia arrancándote hasta el cuero cabelludo,
el azul del llanto, que se atasca
apenas a un abrazo del borde de los ojos.

Viene bien el frío,
la despensa con su rastro de avena y cucarachas,
el reloj extraviado,
el lecho amargo de esta noche sin Prozac,
si tocan a la puerta...

SOPHIE MARÍÑEZ
[FRANCE/DOMINICAN R./USA]

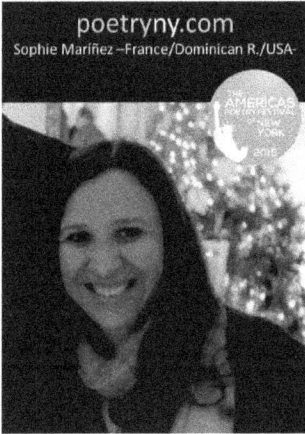

Sophie Maríñez is a scholar and a professor of French and Spanish at the Borough of Manhattan Community College, City University of New York. Born in France and partially raised in the Dominican Republic, she has lived in New York City since 1994. She has worked as an actress, a translator, a journalist, and, from 1997 to 2000, a diplomat for the Dominican Republic in Mexico. She holds a Ph.D. in French from The Graduate Center, City University of New York. Prior to her current position at CUNY, she held a two-year visiting faculty position at Vassar College. Her most recent poems have been published in *Small Axe* and the anthology *Tough Times in America*.

THE HUMPBACK WHALES OF SAMANÁ

Sweet almonds
half-chewed by the sun
fall onto rugged reefs,
mix with dry branches
and leaves aged gold.
The sky wakes
like soft lavender
spreading over
the purple sea.

A siren's cry
calls out in the distance.
From the cosmic womb,
two giant whales spring up
while ahead of them
a coveted mate quietly floats.
A fifty-foot black mass,
she spouts occasional geysers,
echoing the shush of foam
across the serried waves.

Under the sky,
competition begins.
The males' pore-covered jaws
break out toward the sun,
leaping forth
and hunching back,
humping, diving, splashing,
striking the waves
with powerful flukes
until one of them wins
the desired prize.

For hours, day and night,
Howls, shrieks, and moans
make strange water songs;
she sways majestic, slow,
flipping over the surface,
turning over and again,
until the loser is decided,
and she and her winner
smoothly dive to the depths,
away from light
and the curious eye.

TOMÁS MODESTO GALÁN
[DOMINICAN REPUBLIC]

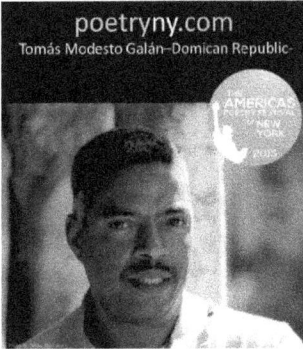

poetryny.com
Tomás Modesto Galán–Domican Republic–

Tomás Modesto Galán. Dominican writer, professor and cultural activist, who has lived in New York since 1986. He holds a Master's degree from Universidad Autonoma de Santo Domingo. Galan has been a Spanish Professor and others courses at the U.A.S.D. In New York, he works at CUNY and Pace University. Currently, he teaches at York College. He is the Cultural Coordinator of the Latino-American Book Festival, Libro Abierto. Some of his works have appeared in several anthologies: Voces de Ultramar, Viajeros del Rocío, Tertuliando, and Brújula Compass 28, de 1998. His book *Los Niños del Monte Edén* was translated into English by the poet Maria Bennett and edited by actor Water Krochmall and poet Rhina Espaillat. He has published: *Los Cuentos de Mount Hope* (novel, 1995, 2nd ed. (2014).); *Los niños del Monte Edén* (short stories, 1998); *Cenizas del Viento* (poetry, 1983); *¿Es popular la poesía de Juan Antonio Alix?* (essay, 1987); *Diario de Caverna* (poetry, 1988); and *Subway* (poetry, 2008). His poetry collection *Amor en bicicleta* was awarded the Premio Letras de Ultramar 2014.

AMOR EN BICICLETA

El suplicio le venda ojos al condenado del placer,
los amantes proveen clavículas, migrañas, no administran el tiempo,
la noche desentierra un orfelinato, incrimina la otra cara del vacío.

Diariamente caen alfileres sobre su claridad, bombas de humo,
Incienso. Una bicicleta rueda sobre la tarde en busca del amor.

Se perdieron puertas, dura demasiado el sol, tardan lunas los cuadernos,
vuelven más estrellas a convocar el salto, la jornada de escondernos
acaricia una brújula descompuesta.

El empeño en destruirnos inaugura suplicios, alumbra sus cadenas,
un surgimiento de hogueras sordas devuelve un perro desnudo
y la mañana desenrosca bastones para caminar a la redonda,
rodar entre corredores ciegos, o niños que bordean un río irrespirable.

A mitad de la razón alguien dinamita el silencio.

Desaparece devorando un piano, sorteados por una libertad absurda
y esa lucha con la luz que los vuelve harapientos, rabiosamente inútiles.

Hoy perdieron los pies, más tarde el amor consumirá el hígado,
después masticará los restos de un pulmón risible pero no amedrentarán
los rayos taciturnos de una bicicleta desventurada que ha perdido el
rumbo.

SILVIA MA. SILLER ARGÜELLO
[MEXICO]

poetryny.com
Silvia Ma. Siller Argüello –Mexico-

Silvia Ma. Siller Argüello de Heller is a poet, translator, communications consultant in philanthropy and Latin America, and cultural promoter. Her first poetry collection, *De Mariposas y Mantis*, won second place in the International Latino Book Award 2015. Her poetry collection Early Morning #5 is a bilingual (English-Spanish) and soon French and Spanish. She has also written and produced two flamenco-theatre creations: *Este nuestro espacio* and *El monólogo de la gitana* that include her poems. She received the Gabriela Mistral, Julia de Burgos and Frida Kalho award by the group Galo Plaza in New York for her contribution to the Latin American culture. She holds a Master's Degree in International and Public Affairs from the Columbia University and has a BA in International Relations from the U. Iberoamericana in Mexico City as well as a Certificate in Latin American Literature. She founded the group fuegodeluna.org, to promote poetry in Spanish in New York. She participates in different recitals, international festivals and book fairs. She has lived in Mexico, Paris and New York and speaks Spanish, English, French, Portuguese and Italian.

POEMBIRTH

In that hollow of light rests a dusk that barely chases its imprint
it pretends to harvest from distance the memories that stalk each
shard of oblivion
a silhouette repeated to exhaustion in the sands
and the waves take over and nest, from its blackest innards
bearing the whole story uphill,
the conception place for the poem that aims to be the fingerprint's
embryo
in its reflection is somewhere else;
pinecone hollow, concealed fire rattle.
In the ocean millions of nothings beat to a single breath
where everything becomes a poem
despite concealed hollows of light
despite the salt in the sands
despite all paths barring its way,
the waves couple with the wisdom of instinct which, from the hollow,
nestles the poem´s
howl

Translation by Walter Krochmal

Parto de poema

En ese hueco de luz reposa un crepúsculo que apenas persigue su
huella
finge cosechar de la distancia los recuerdos que acechan cada pedazo
de olvido
una silueta repetida hasta el cansancio en la arena
y el oleaje se impone y anida desde lo más negro de sí mismo
con toda la historia a cuestas,
es otro el lugar donde se engendra el poema que pretende ser embrión
de la huella en su reflejo,
hueco de bellota, oculto cascabel de fuego.
En el océano se laten millones de nadas en un solo aliento
donde todo se vuelve poema
aunque huecos de luz escondidos,
aunque la sal de la arena,
aunque todos los senderos lo impidan,
las olas copulan la sabiduría del instinto que desde el hueco,
acuna el grito
del poema

ROLANDO PÉREZ
[CUBA]

Rolando Pérez is professor of Spanish and Latin American literature and philosophy at the Romance Languages Department of Hunter College—CUNY. He is the author of numerous publications on the Neo-Baroque, and the relation between literature, the visual arts, and philosophy. He has written on Severo Sarduy, César Vallejo, Alejandra Pizarnik, Octavio Paz, as well as on Bartolomé de Las Casas, Enrique Dussel, Gilles Deleuz & Félix Guattari, Emmanuel Lévinas, and Alain Badiou. Pérez is also the author of a number of literary works, some which have been anthologized in *The Norton Anthology of Latino Literature* (2012). His most recent publication, *Severo Sarduy and the Neo-Baroque Image of Thought in the Visual Arts* was published in 2011 by Perdue University Press. Forthcoming in early 2016 is a bilingual edition of *The Electric Comedy/La comedia eléctrica*, translated by Óscar Curieses, to be published by Amargord Ediciones.

IN THE BEGINNING

I don't remember how I got here. I only know that it hit me one day very suddenly. Perhaps I was born here. I am not quite sure, since there is no one here who speaks my language. In the last few years I have come to realize that I am sinking deeper and deeper into this quicksand. There might have been some signs before that, but I must admit that I never noticed them until recently. After all, how could I have known they were meant for me? A little red light in the night was not enough to deduce anything. Surely, I could have asked someone, but whom? That was the problem from the very beginning. There simply wasn't anyone around. Everyone in the early days spent their lives at the dog races; and only rarely did I hear news of anything different. It was always the same score: 10-1 or 2-11.

Even the temperature changed very little: some degrees up or down, but nothing very drastic. In fact, the temperature of the quicksand has remained rather constant. There might be some minimal fluctuation in the evenings, but nothing to speak of.

Yes, I have tried screaming, I have tried singing, I have tried writing, I have even tried using the Morse Code, but nothing: no response. It almost seems as though someone has cut the wires. The question, of course, is "who?" Then, perhaps no one did. Perhaps they're at the races, and they've forgotten all about me. In the beginning a few people came by, who were nice enough to feed me, but it's been some years since that, and I am no longer certain that I know what they look like, so even if I saw them again, I wouldn't be able to recognize them.

AL PRINCIPIO

No recuerdo cómo llegué hasta aquí. Sólo sé que un día pensé en ello de repente. Tal vez haya nacido aquí. No estoy muy seguro, ya que no hay nadie que hable mi lengua. En los últimos años me he dado cuenta de que me estoy hundiendo cada vez más en esta arena movediza. Puede que haya habido algunas señales antes, pero debo admitir que no me había dado cuenta hasta hace poco. Después de todo, ¿cómo podría haber sabido que eran para mí? Una lucecita roja en la noche no era suficiente para deducir nada. Sin duda, podría haber preguntado a alguien, pero ¿a quién? Ese era el problema desde el principio. Simplemente no había nadie a mi alrededor. Todo el mundo, en esos primeros días, se pasaba la vida en las carreras de perros; y muy raramente se escuchaban noticias sobre algo diferente. Siempre era la misma puntuación: 10-1 o 2-11.

Incluso la temperatura cambiaba muy poco: algunos grados más o menos, pero nada muy drástico. De hecho, la temperatura de la arena movediza se ha mantenido bastante constante. Puede que haya alguna fluctuación mínima por las noches, pero nada de lo que hablar.

Sí, he intentado gritar, he intentado cantar, he intentado escribir, incluso he intentado usar el Código Morse, pero nada: no hay respuesta. Casi parece como si alguien hubiera cortado los cables. La pregunta, por supuesto, es ¿"quién"? Pero quizá nadie lo haya hecho. Quizá estén todos en las carreras y se hayan olvidado de mí. Al principio algunas personas vinieron a verme, personas lo suficientemente bondadosas como para darme de comer, pero han pasado algunos años desde entonces, y ya no estoy seguro de su aspecto, por lo que si los viera de nuevo, no sería capaz de reconocerlos.

Traducción: Nuria Morgado

SEAMUS SCANLON
[IRELAND]

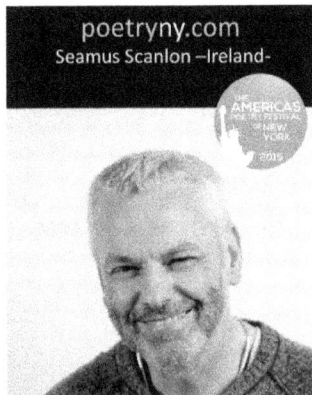

poetryny.com
Seamus Scanlon –Ireland-

Seamus Scanlon is a writer from Galway, Ireland (where Columbus stayed over night before sailing to America!) and is currently based in New York where he is the librarian at City College's Center for Worker Education. His latest book *The McGowan Trilogy* (Arlen House, 2014) was published to coincide with the production of the one act play *Trilogy* in New York by the Cell Theatre Company in September 2014. It won awards for Best Actress, Best Director and Best Design in the annual 1st Irish Theatre Festival. The McGowan Trilogy was also produced in the UK and Ireland during the summer of 2015. His short fiction collection *As Close As You'll Ever Be* (Cairn Press, 2012) will be published in Spanish (Artepoetica Press) under the title *Irlanda en el Corazon* later in 2015. Latest achievements include a month long residency at Dora Marr House in France, and fellowships from The MacDowell Colony and The Centre for Fiction.

THE LONG WET GRASS

The resonance of tires against the wet road is a mantra strong and steady.
The wipers slough rain away in slow rhythmic arcs into the surrounding
blackness.
The rain falls slow and steady, then gusting, reminding me of Galway when
I was a child where Atlantic winds flung broken fronds of seaweed onto the
Prom during high tide. Before the death harmony of Belfast seduced me.
The wind keeps trying to tailgate us. But we keep sailing.
The slick-black asphalt sings on beneath us.
We slow and turn onto a dirt road, the clean rhythm now broken, high
beams tracing tall reeds edging against the road moving rhythmically back
and forth with the wind. No lights now from oncoming cars.
We stop at a clearing.
I open the door.
The driver looks back at me.
The rain on my face is soothing.
The pungent petrol fumes comfort me.
The moon lies hidden behind black heavy clouds.
I unlock the trunk.
You can barely stand after lying curled up for hours.
After a while you can stand straight.
I take the tape from your mouth. You breathe in the fresh air.
You breathe in the fumes.
You watch me. You don't beg. You don't cry. You are brave.
I hold your arm and lead you away from the roadway, into a field, away
from the car, from the others.
The pistol in my hand pointed at the ground.
I stop. I kiss your cheek. I raise the pistol.
I shoot you twice high in the temple.
The coronas of light anoint you. You fall.
The rain rushes to wipe the blood off.
I fire shots into the air.
The ejected shells skip away.
I walk back to the car and leave you there lying in the long wet grass.

LA HIERBA ALTA Y MOJADA

La resonancia de los neumáticos contra la carretera mojada es un mantra fuerte y uniforme.

Los limpiaparabrisas apartan la lluvia con lentos arcos rítmicos hacia la oscuridad circundante.

La lluvia cae fuerte y uniforme, luego en ráfagas que me recuerdan a Galway cuando era niño y los vientos del Atlántico lanzaban las frondas rotas de algas marinas sobre el paseo durante pleamar. Antes de que la armonía de muerte de Belfast me sedujera.

El viento intenta seguirnos de cerca, pero continuamos navegando.

El asfalto de un negro resbaloso continúa su canto bajo nosotros.

Desaceleramos y torcemos hacia un camino de tierra. La limpieza del ritmo se ha roto. Los haces de las luces largas trazan los altos juncos que al borde del camino se mecen al ritmo del viento. Ya no hay luces de carros que vengan de frente.

Nos detenemos en un claro.

Abro la puerta.

El conductor mira atrás, hacia mí.

La lluvia es relajante sobre mi cara.

Los acres vapores de la gasolina me confortan.

La luna permanece escondida detrás de negras y pesadas nubes.

Abro el maletero.

Apenas puedes ponerte de pie luego de haber estado tendido, acurrucado por horas.

Después de un rato te puedes parar derecho.

Retiro la cinta adhesiva de tu boca y aspiras el aire fresco.

Aspiras los vapores.

Me miras. No ruegas. No lloras. Eres valiente.

Te tomo por el brazo y te alejo de la carretera hacia un terreno, lejos del carro, de los otros.

La pistola en mi mano apunta hacia el piso.

Me detengo. Beso tu mejilla. Levanto la pistola.

Te disparo dos veces arriba en la sien.

Los halos de luz te consagran. Caes.

La lluvia corre a apartar tu sangre.

Hago disparos al aire.

Los cartuchos expulsados rebotan lejos de mí.

Camino de regreso al carro y te dejo tendido sobre la hierba alta y mojada.

Translated by Álvaro de Prat

RALPH NAZARETH
[INDIA]

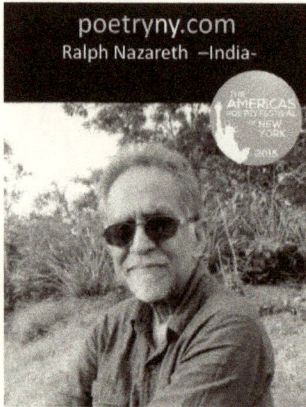

Ralph Nazareth is Professor of English at Nassau Community College on Long Island. For the past ten years he has been a volunteer teacher of creative writing at maximum security prisons in New York State. He is also Managing Editor of Yuganta Press in Stamford and president of Grace Works International, a charitable foundation involved in outreach in the developing world. Nazareth has participated in poetry festivals in India, the Middle East, and in Latin America. His poetry and prose have appeared in books, magazines, and journals in the US and abroad, including most recently in the award-winning collection *Indivisible: An Anthology of Contemporary South Asian American Poetry* and *Multilingual Anthology: The Americas Poetry Festival of New York 2014*. His collection of poems *Ferrying Secrets* was published in 2005 in Hyderabad, India and *Glass: Selected Poems* will be released by El Quirófano Ediciones in Ecuador in the fall of 2015.

PURE INDIAN

Pure is as pure does.
As for the rest there is blending
in ports at the forks of rivers.
Confusion in the synapses.
Enzymes mix as saliva
is exchanged between races.
Sperm and egg conjoin colorblind
in the amniotic dream.
Pure is as death does
as it lies in state beyond division.
Even sworn enemies show up
to lay down a wreathe
though some of the blooms may drip
the blood of your clan.
It's with some difficulty
I say these words:
I am Indian
and wish to be seen as one
composed and taken apart
at the meeting and parting of worlds.

INDIO PURO

La pureza es lo que la pureza hace.
Por lo demás todo es mezcla
en los puertos en el cruce de los ríos.
Confusión de sinapsis
Enzimas mezcladas como saliva
son intercambiada entre las razas.
El esperma y el ovulo se mezclan
en el sueño amniótico sin importar los colores.
La pureza es lo que la muerte hace
mientras descansa en un estado sin división.
Hasta los enemigos jurados vienen
a traer coronas de flores
aunque algunos de los capullos dejen escapar
la sangre de tu clan.
Es con cierta dificultad
que digo estas palabras:
Soy indio
y deseo ser visto como tal
compuesto y descompuesto
en el encuentro y la partida de los mundos.

Traducido del Inglés por Marianela Medrano

José Miguel de la Rosa
[Dominican Republic]

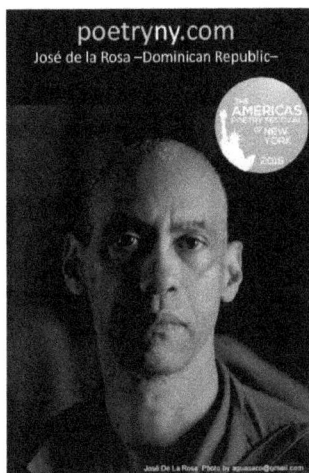

poetryny.com
José de la Rosa −Dominican Republic−

José De La Rosa Photo by aguaseco@gmail.com

José Miguel de la Rosa was born in Santo Domingo, Dominican Republic. The studied Latin American Literature at The City College of New York (CUNY). He was a member of the literary group Pensum.He is also a co-founder of the Hispano/Latino Cultural Center of New York (HLCCNY). He has published the poetry collections Entre *sonrisas y sueños* and *Otra latidud.* Some of his works have been included in anthologies such as *Niveles del imán, La espiga del siglo, Tertuliando, Historias de Washington Heights y otros rincones del mundo, Viajeros del rocío, Noches de vino y rosas* (Obsidiana Press, 2010), *Campo de los patos* (Oviedo, Spain, 2013), *Festival Latinoamericano de Poesia Ciudad de Nueva York 2012: antología* (Urpi Editores/Academia Norteamericana de la Lengua, 2012). He has also published a the play *La loca de la estación Central* (Micielo Ediciones, México, 2010). Ovejita Books will release his new poetry collection entitled *Días infinitos.*

163

MUNDOS POSIBLES

He aquí este sueño
en este azul tinto
de un febrero que se desborda en nieve
Puntualidad de sobremesa con humo
Hablamos de lo que no existe de lo extraño de lo posible
Del otro lado de la pared
[vivimos en una pieza]
unos actores viejos ensayan
una obra de Ibsen
Entre risas alguien mencionó a Edvard Munch
Entonces se produjo un momento de ensueño:
un mundo salido de otro mundo
Hubo manzanas ciruelas peras cocidas a fuego lento
en ron y azúcar moreno
Terminado el postre
nos despedimos entre humo y abrazos
hasta la vuelta
cuando nos vuelva a juntar el destino
Al salir las palabras quedaban flotando en el ambiente.

YOLANDA HERNÁNDEZ
[DOMINICAN REPUBLIC]

poetryny.com
Yolanda Hernández –Dominican Republic–

Yolanda Hernández was born in the Dominican Republic. She is a poet, an actress and vocational and autodidactic painter. In the theatre, she has participated in plays such as *The Vagina Monologues, Deporte Nacional*, a play by Cuban playwright Jesus del Castillo, and in *La Cuesta Magica*, by Dominican playwright Jesus Dante Castillo, plays that were performed in Providence, Rhode Island and Matanzas, Cuba. Her works of literatura have been published in different magazines, local newspapers, and social networks. Part of her poetry has been included in the anthologies, "Solo para Locos volumen II" (Batista-Jakab, Lourdes, 2015) and in "Voces Poéticas Latinas de New England" (Peralta, Luis, Páramo Editorial, EEUU. 2013). "Aroma" is her first published book and has three unedited books including children's literature, narrative, and a bilingual book of poems entitled, *De la ciudad y otras luciérnagas*, dedicated to the city of Providence, Rhode Island.

SANDECES

Quien quita y te quedes conmigo
sin apresurar las horas
domesticando la noche
acortando distancias
caminando por las calles
hostigadas de nostalgia
de esta ciudad dormida
repleta de cuajos y difuntos
de luces quebrantadas
y ebrios pájaros cobrizos.

Quien quita y esta noche
bajo el fino polvo de la luna
te quedes conmigo
inventando sandeces
desgajando los sentidos
sorprendiendo tus labios
hurgando mis adentros
colgándome en tu boca
nadando entre tus aguas
bajando a tus abismos.

No te vayas sin que la noche
quiebre la oculta liviandad
reflejada en el temblor de tus pupilas
quiero mojarme, ahogarme
bogando a la orilla de tu ombligo.

Inventemos sandeces
en las infieles horas
de esta ciudad dormida.

LUIS REYNALDO PÉREZ
[DOMINICAN REPUBLIC]

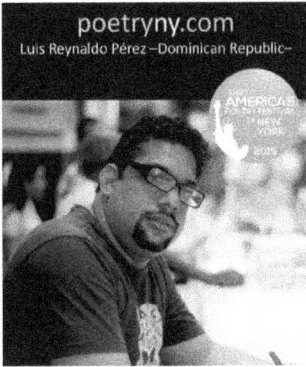

poetryny.com
Luis Reynaldo Pérez –Dominican Republic–

Luis Reynaldo Pérez (Santo Domingo, 1980) poet, editor and cultural activist. He has published *Temblor de lunas* (Santo Domingo: Ediciones de Cultura, 2012, bilingual edition Spanish-Japanese) and *Urbania* (Santo Domingo: Editorial Funglode, 2013). The ebook *Toda la luz* (Santo Domingo: Luna Insomne Editores, 2013,) and the children's book *Lunario* (Santo Domingo: Alfaguara, 2014). He has received, among others, the following awards: Premio único del Premio Funglode de Poesía Pedro Mir 2012 and Premio único del I Concurso Nacional de Haikú 2011.

Minúscula constelación de huesos

Soy el niño que dejó junto al fuego sus dedos tibios. Atardecido bajo sombra de pájaros. Navego en un vaso de estrellas hasta la penumbra enverdecida y herrumbrosa. Desnochecido. ¿Cómo voy a regatear un trozo de luz a esta noche bruta que se cierne en mis huesos? ¿Y esta lluvia escupiendo cuchillos sobre mi cabeza? ¿Y la acuosa mano del silencio desmigajando cada esperanza que pasta en mis ojos? Una tristeza hermosa se arrebola en mis mejillas y sigo despierto en la terrible oscurecencia del insomnio, escuchando la insistencia de una gota de viento en la pared, murmullando una melodía que florece en la luminosa esquina de la memoria. Aquí estoy, cosido a este desamparado de párpados abiertos que me succiona.

ISABEL ESPINAL
[USA/DOMINICAN REPUBLIC]

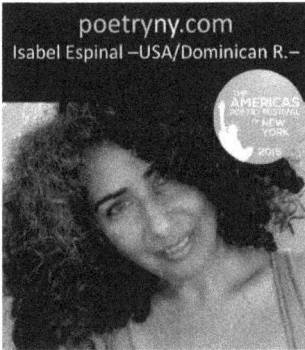

poetryny.com
Isabel Espinal –USA/Dominican R.–

Isabel Espinal was born in New York City in 1964, two years after her parents immigrated from the Cibao countryside in the Dominican Republic. She attended MIT and graduated from Princeton University with a degree in Romance Languages and Literature. She earned a Masters degree in Library and Information Studies from UC Berkeley in 1991 and has been a librarian ever since. She also gave birth to a raised three children, now 22, 20 and 18 years old. In 1993, inspired by feelings of life and mortality inherent in being the mother, Isabel started writing down poetry. She published a chapbook of poetry, *Clean Sheets*, in 1996, as part of a series edited by poet Lourdes Vazquez, and in anthologies such as *Tertuliando / Hanging Out* and an issue of the journal *Callaloo* dedicated to Dominican Literature. Isabel currently works fulltime as a librarian while pursuing a PhD in American Studies with a dissertation on contemporary Dominican women writers in the United States. She grew up in Sunset Park Brooklyn, a short subway ride away from the main venue of the Americas Poetry Festival of New York. Her father had worked as a busboy at Windows on The World, decades before it came down on September 11. Isabel had worked at the Statue of Liberty when she was in high school, taking the ferry from Battery Park. So when she first came to the Americas Poetry Festival in 2014, she reconnected with the spirits that she and her family members had left behind over the years. In 2013-2014 she was President of REFORMA: The National Association to Promote Library and Information Services to Latinos and the Spanish Speaking.

WAIT

I'm sitting here outside of time right now
waiting for you

Inside of time it got very stuffy

I had to get out

I don't know if I've been waiting an hour
or a year

I don't know if I just got here or I have to leave already

I don't want to wait any more but I don't want to leave

Now I'm flying outside of time
I'm jumping
I'm swimming

But I can't change anything out here

I want to change things!

For that I have to go back inside
back inside of time.

ESPERA

Aquí estoy sentada, afuera del tiempo,
esperándote

Dentro del tiempo no había aire

Tuve que salirme de ahí

No sé si he estado esperando una ahora
o un año

No sé si acabo de llegar o si ya me tengo que ir.

No quiero esperar más pero no me quiero ir

Ahora estoy volando fuera del tiempo
Estoy saltando
Estoy nadando

Pero aquí afuera no puedo cambiar nada

¡Quiero hacer cambios!

Para eso tendré que volver adentro
volver adentro del tiempo

JULIET P. HOWARD
[USA]

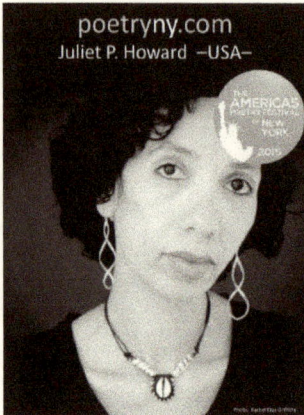

poetryny.com
Juliet P. Howard —USA—

JP Howard a.k.a. Juliet P. Howard is a NY-based poet and Cave Canem graduate fellow. She is the author of SAY/MIRROR, a debut poetry collection published by The Operating System (2015) and a chaplet "bury your love poems here" (Belladonna Collaborative*, 2015). JP curates and nurtures Women Writers in Bloom Poetry Salon and Blog (WWBPS), a forum offering women writers at all levels a venue to come together in a positive and supportive space. WWBPS hosts monthly literary Salons throughout NY. JP is an Alum of the VONA/Voices Workshop. She is a Lambda Literary Foundation Emerging LGBT Voices Fellow, as well as a Cave Canem Fellow in Residence at the Virginia Center for the Creative Arts. She was a finalist in The Feminist Wire's 2014 1st Poetry Contest and in the poetry category for the Lesbian Writer's Fund of Astraea Lesbian Foundation for Justice. Her poems have appeared or are forthcoming in *The Feminist Wire, Split this Rock, Nepantla: A Journal for Queer Poets of Color, Muzzle Magazine, Adrienne: A Poetry Journal of Queer Women, The Best American Poetry Blog, MiPOesias, The Mom Egg, Talking Writing* and Connotation Press.

I AM SELF PORTRAIT

"I paint self portraits because I am so often alone,
because I am the person I know best."
Frida Kahlo

I am alone.
Often I paint portraits of self.
I am the person I paint.
I am self portrait because I know best.

Often I paint portraits of self.
I paint often because
I know self best.
I paint alone.

I am the person I paint.
I know,
I am alone
because I am self portrait.

I am self portrait because I know best.
I know I paint,
because I am alone.
Alone, I am often best.

MARYAM ALIKHANI
[IRAN/USA]

poetryny.com
Maryam Alikhani –Iran/USA–

Maryam Alikhani is an Iranian-American poet, a translator, and an adjunct instructor of English Composition and Technical Writing at CUNY. She graduated with the degree of MFA in Creative Writing from the City College of NY, and currently is working on her doctoral research in Teaching of English at Columbia University. She writes her poems in English, Farsi, and Spanish and sometimes with a mixture of words in Turkish, Kurdish, and Arabic which are her passive languages. Her poetry has appeared in *Esque Mag*, *Poetry in Performance*, *Promethean*, *The Poetry of Yoga* as well as several periodicals in Tehran.

RECOMPOSITION

My poems do not promise anything
I only compose my world as it happens.
Kiss me word by word
Touch me line by line
I do not need to mean, but to be, like a poem.

Read me in every context that melts on your tongue.
I speak the language of the moment.
Track me; I have no past.
Trust me, there is no future.
Do not disturb my imagery of the universe.

My red planet is a rolling stone
That does not revolve around any sun.
It crosses your system once in a blue moon
And does not obey the laws of your physic–
Not denying the chemistry between us!

Join me in my oval orbit
Ovulating stars that have no gravity
Galaxies that have no memories of big bang.
Do not try to swallow me like a black hole
Or you will always remain dark.

We can destroy the old world in six days
Take a rest on the seventh day
Then order a new genesis for two infinite gods
Absolutely guilt free.

My cosmology has no chronology
It just happens at this moment.
I am not playing Emily Dickinson
Or Forough Farokhzad
I am just trying to recompose myself.

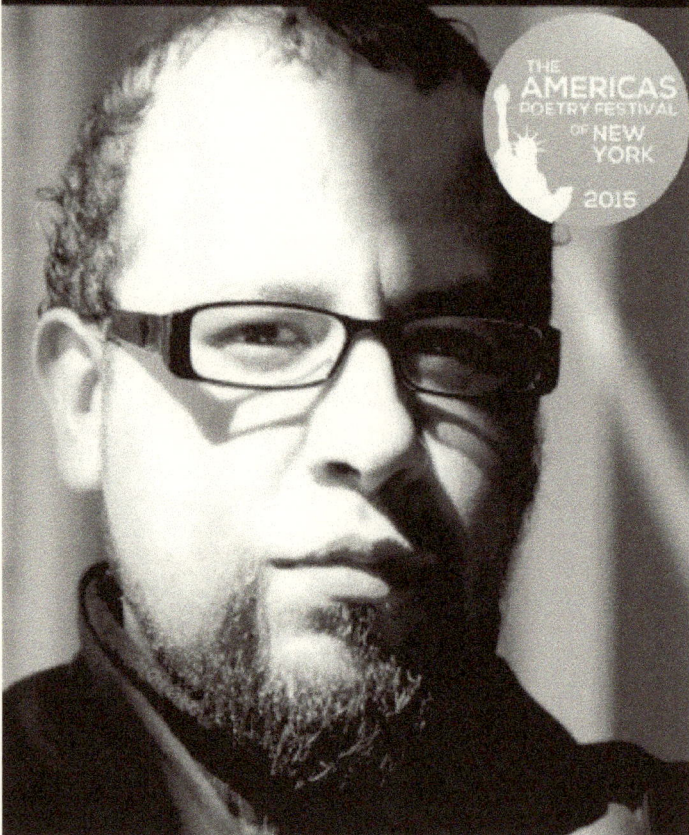

poetryny.com
Honoring the memory of poet
William Beltrán (AKA William Akcoo)
1973-2011

THE
AMERICAS
POETRY FESTIVAL
OF NEW
YORK
2015

THE AMERICAS POETRY FESTIVAL OF NEW YORK 2015

HONORS THE MEMORY OF POET WILLIAM BELTRÁN

William Beltrán was born in Bogotá in 1973 and passed away in 2011. He received a BA in Art from the National University of Colombia and a Master in Aesthetics at Universidad Complutense de Madrid. He pursued doctoral studies both at U Complutense and the Institut für Philosophie of the University of Bremen, Germany. He was a specialist in the philosophy of Nietzsche and a member of the Spanish Association of Nitzchean Studies. His published poetry collections are *Por Ultratumba y de los Poemas Cansados* (1993), *Versos para el Inculpado* (1999) and *La tiniebla de la culpa* (2008).

Poems by William Beltrán, translated from Spanish by Carlos Aguasaco.

Es – QUIZOFRENIA

Cuando las pupilas
ensanchan los tesoros
del capitán
de mi naufragio.

S-CHIZOPHRENIA

When the pupils
enlarge the treasures
of my shipwreck's
captain

SEMBLANTE

Acaecía en la cogulla,
sentado,
traslúcido.
En sus rostros de niño
inhumaba en Ultratumba
la sobreviviente castidad de la sonrisa:
caleidoscopio de pupilas;
como profeta de las máscaras,
pendía del hilo de la araña.
-De ese arácnido complejo que
llaman: la risa.

COUNTENANCE

He stayed under the hood,
seated,
translucent.
In their childlike faces
he buried in the afterlife
the persistent chastity of a smile:
kaleidoscope of pupils;
like the prophet of disguises
hanging from a spider's silk.
Hanging from that complex arachnid
they call: laughter.

DECLAMACIÓN

> *"Que como yo muere en soledad,*
> *y que el tiempo, ese viejo calumnioso,*
> *con su ala torpe hiere cada día"*
> Ch. Baudelaire

En el ademán de sus manos,
escapando furtivamente tras los brazos,
se intuye "un gesto camaleónico del verso";
como si en ellas un ritual bélico,
prescindiendo de la voluptuosidad del tiempo.
-Soloquizástalvezaguardara
latente,
el réquiem tumefacto…
de la mutilación.

DECLAMATION

"Which, like me, dies in solitude,
And which Time, that contemptuous old man,
wounds each day with his rough wing…"
Baudelaire

In their hand gestures,
Secretly escaping after the arms,
one can sense "a chameleonic gesture of the verse;"
as if they embodied a bellicose ritual,
giving up on time's voluptuousness.
-Onlyperhapsmaybeawaited
latent
the swollen requiem…
of mutilation.

ARTE POÉTICA

Cuando después de tres o cuatro sismos,
mis laberintos enmudecen
entre algunos abismos cortos,
no tan cortos como las palabras:
intento telarañas retóricas.
Mi problema es despertar sin piso,
como Pegaso o como Ícaro.
El papel –sofisma es
capaz de arrancar un llanto,
o una canción de cuna;
dejo siluetas marcadas en lo que clavo en el tiempo -efímero
enemigo-.
Y entonces:
soy quijote de grafismos,
mi Dulcinea…
Cuando vuele otro poema,
como Pegaso,
o como Ícaro.

ART POETICS

When after three or four tremors
my labyrinths become quiet
In between some short abysms,
not as short as words:
I attempt to make rhetoric webs.
My problem is waking up groundless,
like Pegasus or Icarus.
The paper—a sophism
able to yank a cry,
or a lullaby;
I leave marked silhouettes in what I nail to time, ephemeral
enemy-.
Then,
I am a Quixote of graphemes,
my Dulcinea…
when a new poem flies away
like Pegasus
or Icarus.

DE POETA A POETA

Asimismo, desprevenido
solíais aguantar por horas agotando el camino.
Vaciando de vez en cuando los bolsillos.
Ojeabais de memoria algún libro,
o de pronto, angustiado
sorbíais café sobre una mesa.
Tendíais también los ojos
en el suelo rojizo – color pereza –
presintiendo lágrimas, ausentes siempre por vehemencia.
Ni hablar de las puntillas de los dedos sin cigarros.
Ni de uno que otro
pensar en no pensar en la lascivia;
arrodillabais luego bajo la sombra de un arbusto,
o molestabais con sentires los mortales.
Pensabais en Dios, de vez en cuando.
Y prometíais el vicio de arrojaros por las calles agrisadas.
¡Pero no os perdono:
porque nunca ,
del jamás !
se os ocurría pensar, como yo…
en Poesía.

POET TO POET

Likewise, unprepared
You usually resist for hours consuming the road.
Emptying your pockets occasionally.
By memory, you would glance over a book
or suddenly, distressed
you would sip coffee on a table.
You would also fix your sight
on the reddish ground –lazy color-
anticipating tears, always absent for vehemence
not to mention the cigarless fingertips.
Or thinking about
not thinking about lust;
You would then kneel under the shadow of a bush
Or would bother mortals with feelings.
You would think of God, occasionally,
You would promise to take on the grayish streets.
But I do not forgive you,
for you never ever
dared to think, as I do...
of Poetry.

A SOLAS

Tomé su ropa sucia
y como es obvio:
la boté por la ventana.
No tuvo dinero para comprarse un cuerpo.
Ni daban posada
en cualquier nombre.
Así es que, no se fue,
aquí,
hay alguien…
mirándome al espejo.

ALONE

I took his dirty clothes
and obviously
threw them out the window.
He didn't have money to buy himself a body.
Nor did they offer refuge
in any name.
Thus, he did not leave,
there is someone…
here,
watching me from inside the mirror.

El "rictus" del payaso

Invisible significa,
divisible en enésimos fragmentos de aire
que otros no quieren respirar.
Invisible significa,
El reflejo del rostro, en otro
que no inmuta mueca alguna.
El humorismo es invisible
al más alto nivel de intromisión.
El eco, jugando a necio donde no existe
respuesta alguna. Con humor.
En escena:
Un payaso autor (el niño necesario).
La cuerda del saltimbanqui: el escenario.
La cuerda, fina y tensa
es el trazo seguro de la ciencia nauseabunda,
el impoluto rastro del "pensar correcto".
La raya bajo el nombre
que obliga a firmar —y afirmar—.
La risa del payaso es invisible…
No acontece para el otro,
como la risa del autor.
Si acontece: es apariencia;
Vaho,
humo;
Estupor.
Invisible significa, no por esto,
no presencia sobre la cuerda suspensa.
Vulgar "sostén", ella, amargada vieja necia
que resiste envejecer.
Hoy hay función en el rostro,
como siempre hay humor.
Atiborrado el auditorio,
pletórico el bufón.
Invisible significa,
que la gente nunca sabe,
que el payaso vive ebrio
y desde siempre un saltimbanqui.

THE CLOWN'S GRIN

Invisible means,
divisible in a zillion fragments of air
that others refuse to breathe.
Invisible means,
mirroring your face onto another
gesture-less one.
Humor is invisible
to the highest level of intrusion.
The echo, playing dumb where there are
no responses. With humor.
In scene:
A clown author (the necessary child).
The acrobat's rope: the stage.
The rope, fine and tense,
Is the line of the nauseating science,
the unpolluted mark of "correct thought".
The line under your name
Forcing you to sign –and to affirm-.
The clown's laughter is invisible…
It does not exist for the other,
Just like the author's laughter.
If it takes place: it is only apparent;
Mist,
Smoke,
Stupor.
Invisible means, not because of it,
No presence on the tightrope.
Vulgar "brassiere", her, bitter old woman
who resists aging.
Today, there will be a show in this face,
as there is always humor.
A fully packed auditorium,
the jester, plethoric.
Invisible means,
That the people never know
The clown is always drunk
And has always been an acrobat.